CW00554022

Exile From Argentina

*A Jewish Family
and the Military Dictatorship
(1976–1983)
(2nd Edition)*

Exile From Argentina

*A Jewish Family
and the Military Dictatorship
(1976–1983)
(2nd Edition)*

by

Eduardo D. Faingold

INFORMATION AGE PUBLISHING, INC.
Charlotte, NC • www.infoagepub.com

Library of Congress Cataloging-in-Publication Data

Paperback: 979-8-88730-459-5
Hardcover: 979-8-88730-460-1
E-Book: 979-8-88730-461-8

First published in Argentina under the title *Diáspora y exilio. Crónica de una familia argentina* by Ediciones Al Margen, 2006.

Translated by Renata Madinger, Noam Faingold, and Eduardo D. Faingold

Copyright © 2024 Information Age Publishing Inc.

Printed in the United States of America

In memory of my father, Enrique Faingold (1925–2012)

Contents

PART 1

An Argentine Family

PART 2

An Argentine Kid

Preface to the 2nd Edition

It has been more than 15 years since the first edition of *Exile From Argentina*, in which I tell the story of my ancestors who emigrated in the 19th century from Byelorussia and Bessarabia to Argentina as a part of the Baron de Hirsch's emigrant wave that established farming villages in the provinces of Santa Fé and Buenos Aires, Moises Ville and Médanos (on my mother's side) and Algarrobos, Roberts, and Carlos Casares (on my father's). The book also narrates incidents that happened to my family in La Plata and Buenos Aires as a result of state terrorism during the last military dictatorship in Argentina (1976–1983): the home invasions, the murders, the bombs; and how, in October of 1976, the family left Argentina for Israel with the help of the Jewish Agency.

I dedicate a great part of the book to narrating my family's challenges in Israel; my brothers and I as teenagers living apart from my parents and baby sister, scattered in different cities and *kibbutzim* all over Israel; the uprooting, loss, and lack of adaptation to an unfamiliar environment; the psychological, social, and economic problems of our family; living every day's reality in a very different culture, struggling to communicate in a new language. I narrate significant events in my life at the *mechina* (preparatory) of the Hebrew University in Jerusalem and at several *kibbutzim* where I worked and studied Hebrew until April of 1978 when I left Israel for Denmark. I tell about my experiences in Denmark, where I lived for nearly a year as a refugee, and my return to Argentina in 1979 to participate in mandatory military service as required by law. I write about my experiences in the Ar-

Exile From Argentina: A Jewish Family and the Military Dictatorship (1976–1983), 2nd Edition, pages ix–xiv.
Copyright © 2024 by Information Age Publishing
www.infoagepub.com

gentine military (1979–1980), as a conscript in the Argentine Marines, 3rd Marine Battalion (BIM3), in the middle of the Dirty War (1976–1983); and I recall conversations I had with Argentine officers and NCOs, who openly expressed their antisemitic beliefs, but who, paradoxically, also showed great respect and admiration for the Israeli Army and the State of Israel: "*un país que pega fuerte*" (a country that hits hard).

In April 1980, when I was released from the military, I no longer saw a place for myself in Argentina, in a country where films and books were getting banned on a daily basis by Señor Paulino Tato, the official government censor, and where people could be killed or disappeared at any time because of their political ideas. Thus, a few days after I was released from military service, I applied for a new Argentine passport, and on May 24, 1980, I returned to Israel. This time nobody forced me to leave the country. I left because I wanted to, because I felt that I didn't belong in Argentina any longer.

Why Israel? Why not go back to Denmark, where my then girlfriend lived? The truth is, returning to Israel felt like going back to a place where I could have some sense of belonging. I still remember the feeling of happiness arriving at the airport in Tel-Aviv and seeing my brother Roberto and my friends Analía and Dani who were waiting for me at the airport. Only two years had passed since I left Israel for Denmark and Argentina, but it felt as if a whole lifetime full of intense experiences had passed!

At the time of my arrival in Israel on May 29, 1980, the headlines of the Israeli Spanish language newspaper *Aurora* noted a close "Aeroflot-Argentine airlines collaboration" and the "Priority of the USSR for Argentine meat." For someone fresh out of the anti-communist hysteria created by the Argentine military during the dictatorship, these were amazing facts. Another headline in the newspaper stated: "The kidnapping of Eichmann—The film is banned in Buenos Aires." The headline left no doubt that antisemitic beliefs had taken hold among members of the military junta, which a few months later would allow a large-scale media campaign against the Jewish community of Argentina to be carried out. Not surprisingly, a January 1981 headline in the same newspaper noted a "wave of antisemitism in Argentina." The article went into detail about the violent antisemitic incidents that were taking place at the time in Buenos Aires: bombs at the Guerzenstein Orthodox Seminary; in the ORT schools of Yatay Street; at the Bialik school in Aguirre Street; at the Jerusalem synagogue and its annexed school. The article also mentioned the large amounts of Nazi literature that were being sold in newspaper stands in Argentina at the time, and emphasized the abusive vitriolic attacks on Jewish participants by the journalist Llamas de Madariaga in the Videoshow TV program: "Are you Jewish or Argentine?"

"Why are the Jews so greedy?" "Why are there no poor Jews?" The article in *Aurora* concluded with a statement about the ill-treatment and violations of human rights of Argentine Jews in the jails of the dictatorship, pointing to a recent report by the Inter-American Commission on Human Rights that noted the "systematic use of torture" and "the killing of men and women" by the dictatorship.

In Israel, the above mentioned events did not go unnoticed, and notably, they were also debated in the Knesset (the Israeli parliament). Accordingly, a headline in *Aurora* in June 1981 reported that "Sheli (a left-wing party) asks for a break with Argentina." Specifically, the article noted that following the disclosures of journalist Jacobo Timerman, who had been kidnapped by the military and was now living in exile in the United States, about antisemitism in the jails of the dictatorship,

> Meir Pail (a member of the Knesset representing Sheli) called for the immediate breakdown of relations with a country where Jews are killed for their status as such. (...) Pail criticizes Mota Gur and Itzhak Rabin of the Ma'arakh (a center-left party) for having agreed to visit that country. (*Aurora*, June 18, 1981)

Another headline in *Aurora*, on April 27, 1982, noted the English landing in South Georgia to evict Argentine military personnel there, which resulted in the pointless war between Argentina and the United Kingdom in the Malvinas/Falkland Islands (April 2, 1982–June 14, 1982). Coincidentally, at the same time that the Malvinas/Falklands War was taking place in the South Atlantic, Israel also got involved in a senseless and bloody war in Lebanon (1982–2000).

Soon after arriving in Israel I got a job at the Jerusalem Hilton and moved to an apartment in an old building at the corner of Jaffa road and King George street, right in the middle of downtown Jerusalem. In October 1980, I was awarded a scholarship from the Israeli government to study modern languages at the Hebrew University of Jerusalem, and quit my job at the Hilton. A few weeks later, I met my wife Sonia, who grew up in Israel after emigrating with her family from São Paulo, Brazil. Not long after we met, Sonia moved in with me to the apartment I rented in downtown Jerusalem. We shared the apartment with Marcos, an Argentine exile who had been kidnapped by the military in Argentina and later released thanks to the intervention of his father who was an important leader of the Jewish community in Buenos Aires and a well-known person in Argentina and the United States. At that time, Sonia began her doctoral studies in neurobiology at the Hebrew University, and I started studying for a bachelor's degree in English linguistics and French literature. About a year later, on June 24, 1981, we got married. I remember that, at great expense, my mother came from Argentina to be with us at the wedding, while my father and my sister Paula stayed behind in Argentina. My brothers Roberto and Jorge, and a number of my Argentine friends, who were also attending university in Israel at the time, came to the wedding. A few months later, we moved to an apartment in the dorms for married students at the Hebrew University, where we lived for about year. In 1983, we bought an apartment in the Jerusalem neighborhood of Armon Hanatziv, and on September 8, 1984, our son Noam was born. In 1985, after I graduated from Hebrew University with a BA in English linguistics and French language and literature, the Israeli Ministry of Interior refused to renew my temporary residence permit, and I was left with no choice but to report for induction into the Israeli army or to leave the country. Having served as a conscript in the Argentine military only a few years earlier, the idea of being drafted once again into another army did not appeal to me. To my surprise, however, I was not inducted into the Israeli army due to a medical condition which exempted me from being drafted but not from volunteering.

Since my arrival in Israel in 1980, until I finished my undergraduate degree, I mostly worked at jobs which felt boring and alienating: at the Jerusalem Hilton (first as a pool attendant and later as a switchboard operator); cleaning buildings; making metal plates for printing presses; as a security guard at a hostel for new immigrants; as a cashier at the university bookstore; and at the front desk at the Diplomat hotel. By contrast, at the Hebrew University I enjoyed studying linguistics and literature and writing academic essays. I had the opportunity to study semantics with Robert Lees, a world-famous expert in Chomskyan linguistics. At the French department I studied French literature with Fernande Bartfeld, a well-known scholar of the philosopher Albert Camus, and took a number of master classes in deconstructivism and narratology with visiting philosopher and literary critic Jacques Derrida and film director and novelist Alain Robbe-Grillet.

After completing my bachelor's degree in English and French at the Hebrew University, I decided to pursue a master's degree in English linguistics and to become a language teacher. As an Master's student in English linguistics at the Hebrew University I took advanced courses on bilingualism and child language acquisition with Professor Itzhak Schlesinger of the psychology department, a world-renowned psycholinguist, and in language variation and linguistic theory with my future mentor, Professor C.J. Bailey, Director of the Institute of English and Linguistics at the Technical University of Berlin, who was teaching at the English Department of the Hebrew of the University as a visiting professor at the time. In July 1988, I graduated cum laude with a thesis on the phonological development of multilingual children. At that time, I started teaching English to Hebrew-speaking children in Israeli schools, first as a substitute teacher in an elementary school, and later as a high school teacher in several Israeli cities: the Amal technical school in Beit Shemesh, the school at the Ayanot youth village in central Israel, and the ORT Kennedy school in Jerusalem. I also taught English to a class of Portuguese-speaking children who came from Brazil to finish their high school studies in Ayanot, and Spanish to an American class of English-speaking children who came for their 11th grade year in Jerusalem. I enjoyed teaching languages in high school and I was becoming quite good at it, especially at teaching English to children of socially deprived backgrounds. In October of 1988, C.J. Bailey invited me to study language variation and creole linguistics with professors Karl Maroldt and Freddie Jones, who were teaching linguistics at his institute in Berlin. At that time, I had started to think about the possibility of applying Bailey's theory of language variation to the study of child language acquisition, creolization, and historical change for my doctoral dissertation, using the comprehensive database on child language acquisition by trilingual children, that I had collected for my MA thesis.

In 1989 I started my doctoral studies in linguistics at Tel-Aviv University, under the supervision of Professor Ruth Berman, a pioneer in the field of child language acquisition, with a focus on psycholinguistics, creolistics, and historical linguistics. At that time I also landed my first academic job, teaching Spanish in the Department of Foreign Languages at Tel-Aviv University. In 1989 I won my first research grant, from the DAAD (the German Academic Exchange Service), to travel to Germany, from August to December of 1989, to do research for my doctoral dissertation at the Technical University of Berlin under the mentorship of Professor Bailey. At that time I also started to receive my first invitations to give academic talks at universities and research institutes, by Jürgen Meisel at the Romance Languages Seminar at the University of Hamburg and by Shlomo Izre'el at the research seminar of the Linguistics Department at Tel Aviv University. These were exciting times, as I was coming up with new research ideas and was also presenting my work at important academic venues, getting feedback and receiving encouragement from professional linguists.

In 1990 Sonia was offered a post-doctoral position at the UCLA Brain Research Institute in Los Angeles, and I was invited to be affiliated as a visiting scholar with the Department of Applied Linguistics at UCLA, under the mentorship of Professor Roger Andersen, an expert on the historical development of Papiamento, a Spanish/Portuguese Caribbean creole which was focal to my doctoral dissertation. Thus, on September 5, 1990, a day before my 32nd birthday, we moved to the Westwood area of Los Angeles where we lived for the next two years. In 1992 I was awarded a PhD degree in linguistics, and received an academic excellence award from Tel Aviv University for my doctoral dissertation on language acquisition, creolization, and historical change. Soon after that we moved to Stony Brook, New York, where Sonia was hired to do post-doctoral research in neurobiology at the Howard Hughes Medical Institute, and I was invited to be affiliated as a visiting scholar with the Department of Linguistics, to do post-doctoral work under the mentorship of Professor Mark Aronoff, a well-known scholar in morphology. At that time, I also obtained a dual position as adjunct professor of Hebrew at the Department of Comparative Literature and Spanish at the department of Hispanic Languages and Literatures. In 1995 I was offered and accepted a full-time tenure track position as assistant professor of Spanish at the University of Tulsa in Oklahoma, where I rose through the ranks of the university to become tenured associate professor in 2002 and full professor in 2014.

Nearly thirty years have passed since Sonia, Noam, and I settled down in Tulsa, Oklahoma. I, working as a college professor and Sonia, after earning a second doctorate in clinical Psychology from the University of Tulsa, as a bilingual therapist. Noam left home after finishing high school at Booker T. Washington Highschool in Tulsa, earning a bachelor's degree in music at the University of Tulsa, followed by a master's degree in music from New York University and a doctorate in music composition from King's College London. Noam currently lives in Washington, D.C., where he works as a high school music director and composer. My brother Roberto and his family moved from Israel to São Paulo, Brazil, in 1990, while both their children emigrated to Australia after graduating from university in Brazil. My brother Jorge lives in Oslo, Norway, with his family since the mid-1980s, which now includes three daughters and two grandchildren, all Norwegian born and bred. In 2020 my sister Paula and her family emigrated from Israel to Stockholm, Sweden. My father, Enrique, died in 2012 in Argentina, and about a year later, my mother moved to Israel. And so it goes. At the end of the first quarter of the 21st century, the descendants of my ancestors who emigrated to Argentina from Byelorussia and Bessarabia at the turn of the 19th century to escape the violence of the Russian pogroms are now scattered in five continents, living their lives in cultures as varied as those of the United States, Brazil, Israel, Norway, Sweden, and Australia.

Finally, a selection of photos and documents of the author and his family are featured in an appendix at the end of the book.

EDF

Tulsa, Oklahoma, April 2023

Prologue

Los viejos amores que no están
La ilusión de los que perdieron
Todas las promesas que se van
Y los que en cualquier guerra se cayeron
Todo está guardado en la memoria
Sueño de la vida y de la historia

—León Gieco, *La memoria*

This is a chronicle of my family's experiences that took place before, during, and after the last military dictatorship in Argentina (1976–1983). I have used my diaries, interviews recorded in Argentina, Uruguay, and Israel, documents and pictures given to me by my family and friends and have studied the works of political scientists, historians and journalists to write this book. As much as is possible, I have avoided the use of scholarly quotes in the text in order to facilitate its reading. This is simply a literary device, and the sources that were consulted appear in the bibliography at the end.

I begin this book with my family's history from the time when they immigrated to Argentina at the end of the 19th century. Then, using my family's history as a background, I discuss my family's experience before my parents' decision to move to Israel in 1976, the decision I made to live by myself in Denmark towards the beginning of 1978, my return to Argentina at the beginning of 1979 to comply with military service at Battalion 3 of the Marine Infantry, and my return to Israel in 1980.

Exile From Argentina: A Jewish Family and the Military
Dictatorship (1976–1983), 2nd Edition, pages xv–xviii.
Copyright © 2024 by Information Age Publishing
www.infoagepub.com

During the seven years of the Argentine dictatorship, over thirty thousand people "disappeared" or were murdered by military and paramilitary groups. Approximately two million Argentines went into exile to avoid becoming casualties of the state-sponsored terrorism. Just like the "disappeared," the exiles were also victims of the "Dirty War" of the military against its own country. I think it is important to safeguard the stories of those years during the military repression, and to reproduce testimonies of the damage caused to the victims, including those who left to avoid being murdered by the military. The object of this book is to contribute to the collective memory of Argentina and the concept of *Never Again*, so that this idea can become more of a reality than a dream.

I wrote this book because I thought it would be futile to try to bring these military men to justice in court for the damage, losses and hardships caused to my family during the dictatorship. The losses and difficulties are many: the bewilderment of having to leave the country suddenly in 1976, my family's dispersal throughout the world, the unspoken feeling from friends and family that "there must be a reason for this," that I could be "myself" in Argentina, but could not be that person outside of the country, living at the mercy of Argentine and foreign consulates, immigration agents and bureaucrats, adjusting to different rhythms of life, work and schooling, dealing with neighbors, colleagues and others who have different customs and traditions and for years having an irrational fear of uniformed police officers or soldiers when passing them in the street.

For those like my family, who were part of the middle class, it was very hard to adapt to the economic problems and ask for help. These problems include having children, nieces and nephews, and grandchildren who are not Argentine and who do not speak Spanish or speak it poorly, losing one's roots when one no longer knows one's home, losing one's language, the difficulty of talking and writing about a country in which one no longer resides and in a language one no longer speaks in daily life. The most impossible task was getting used to living in Argentina again after years of living outside of the country.

There were benefits too, though. Learning other languages, cultures and customs, being able to read books which were banned during the dictatorship, or to access information and publications which the Argentines did not have or could not obtain, being able to develop personal projects relating to one's work and studies, having the chance to return to Argentina from the so-called "first world" in order to work on professional projects between the native country and the adopted one and, of course, being lucky to still be alive, having been saved from torture or death during the military dictatorship.

It is hard to come back and not be able to recognize the places where one had grown up. I was shocked, for instance, when I discovered that several of the cafes, bars and other places that I had frequented growing up in La Plata and Buenos Aires were no longer there.

I have very good memories of having spent hours alone or with friends in the cafe Don Julio, where I could skip school on the rainy days and spend the afternoon reading, drinking hot chocolate and eating sandwiches. In the cinema Belgrano, today a parking lot, they would let us in when we were younger than 18 to see R-rated movies, and I would go there when I skipped school with my friend Toledo, a classmate who became ill and passed away a year before finishing high school. In the cinema Select, today an Evangelist church, we would go see rock movies and art cinema. I saw the movies *Woodstock* and *Phantom of the Paradise* there several times, and also all the films of Fellini, Visconti and Antonioni. At the Club Atenas I saw Spinetta, Sui Generis, Vox Dei, Pappo and other famous Argentinean rock bands. There were also the arcade and foosball tables in Cáritas, with its lights always dimmed, where I could spend all day playing pinball.

I remember Libraco, a bookstore where one could buy books on economics and revolutionary politics, which were difficult to find in other bookstores in La Plata. There was also a bookstore (although I forget its name) on 49th Street across the street from the Rocha mall, where I bought science fiction books from the Minotauro collection, and Argentine and Latin American literature from Losada publications, and where I also went to listen to rock records which I could not afford to buy.

In Buenos Aires there was a bar called Los Pinos on Corrientes Street, where I would join Alberto and other local musicians to discuss music.

Some of these places may have disappeared over time through normal means, and as the consequences of the development of a big city. Other places such as Cáritas, the late night movie theater and the bar Los Pinos, where as teenagers we would freely get together in the time before the military dictatorship of 1976, which I am sure were casualties of the dictatorship. It is clear that many of the public places of La Plata and Buenos Aires that I would go to as a young child and teenager—the El Parlamento café in La Plata and the La Opera and La Paz cafes in Buenos Aires, the zoo and the museum of La Plata, the bookstores and movie theaters on the streets Corrientes, Florida, Lavalle and Santa Fe in Buenos Aires—are still there.

There are millions of us in the same situation: Argentines who had to leave the country after many generations there. As this book demonstrates, my family had been in Argentina since the end of the 19ᵗʰ century and for many years had farmed and ranched, had contributed to industry, to commerce and the liberal professions, much more so than the destructive military groups who caused such incredible damage to the country and its people.

* * *

Thirty years after the dictatorship: we were, we are and forever will be in Argentina.

EDF

Tulsa, Oklahoma, August, 2006

PART 1

An Argentine Family

The Maternal Family

¿Cómo crees que vinieron?
Vinieron con los bolsillos vacíos y las manos desnudas
Para trabajar con todas sus fuerzas
Y a desbrozar un sol ingrato

–Charles Aznavour, *Los inmigrantes*

The ancestors of my maternal grandmother Ana Volpin de Turkenich, the Teplitz and the Volpin families, left their town in the region of Grodno, in Byelorussia, on the 4th of January of 1902. They departed from the port of Libava, on the Baltic Sea, headed towards Argentina. They traveled with a second group of immigrants coming from the Grodno region which was organized by the pioneer of the Jewish immigration in Argentina, Noé Cociovich. The Teplitz family and the Volpin family were two of the families who founded Moisesville in the province of Santa Fé. It was one of the most important Jewish colonies of the Jewish Colonization Association (JCA) in Argentina, property of the businessman Mauricio Hirsch. In Moisesville they began growing alfalfa and producing milk and the families each received lots of approximately 100 to 150 acres of land.

Besides the Volpin and the Teplitz families, other families that founded Moisesville included the Reizins, the Ekimovskys, the Ziskandovichs, the Sheinis, the Zak-Guershteins, the Kalers, the Abelyanskys, the Ploschuks, the Berkovichs, the Torgovniks, the Mishkins, the Pribulskys, the Zagonts, the Dubrovskys, the Busels, the Kletskys, the Abramchiks, the Rinlands, the

Exile From Argentina: A Jewish Family and the Military
Dictatorship (1976–1983), 2nd Edition, pages 3–8.
Copyright © 2024 by Information Age Publishing
www.infoagepub.com

Lyskovskys, the Kuzevitskys, the Tenenbaums, the Lifshitzs, the Rubins, the Nahts, the Pruzanskys, the Shusters and the Rinskys.

In 1906 my great-great-grandparents, Jaim Teplitz and Abraham Volpin, along with other colonists, which included Bernardo Radovitzky, Marcos Bernstein, Moises Elman, Salomon Sheinis, Zalman Tujsnaider among others, got into an argument with the JCA due to droughts, floods, and swarms of locusts, but also because the contracts signed with the JCA contained clauses which, for example, prohibited them to give their land to their children. Due to this disagreement, my ancestors and other colonists—rebels who were ready to fight for their rights—left Moisesville. These Jewish families purchased land in the southern part of the province of Buenos Aires from a landlord, and there they founded the Médanos colony, a few kilometers away from the city of Bahía Blanca. After working very hard on clearing the land they had purchased, they at first dedicated themselves to growing grains, alfalfa, oatmeal, wheat and then later to raising cattle. My great-grandfather Samuel Volpin won many prizes for the high quality wheat he grew on his land. Even today, the Volpins dedicate themselves to growing crops and raising cattle in Médanos. My cousin Samuel Volpin continues with the traditions of my maternal ancestors: farmers, dedicating themselves to raising cattle.

Some of my ancestors from this branch of the maternal side of my family took different paths. According to my mother, my great-grandmother's brother, Mashe Teplitz de Volpin, was a captain in the Argentine Army. He was one of the few Jewish people who were promoted to such a high position in the history of the Argentine Army; this was long before the 1930s when the Jews could not follow a military career in the country. Of course, until the abolition of military service in Argentina in 1995, many young Jews, including my family members and myself, were enlisted in the Armed Forces, due to the required military service.

Another one of my ancestors, David Volpin, my grandmother Ana's brother, emigrated to the Ein Hashlosha kibbutz in 1948, in the Negev desert in the recently created State of Israel. In 1951, David was killed by a group of Arabs who tried to steal his herd of sheep. David is buried in the Ein Hashlosha cemetery and, in his honor; the members of the kibbutz placed his picture in the *moadon* (club). Up until very recently, a commemorative plate with his name could be found in the United Israelite Youth Cultural Center (*Centro de Cultura Juventud Unida Israelita*), the community center of the Médanos community. It is a shame that today only three Jewish families remain in Médanos, and that the community center had to be sold to the Unión Cívica Radical (a political party). David Volpin's commemorative plate was moved to a monolith in the Jewish cemetery of Médanos which is dedicated to the six million Jews who were murdered by the Nazis during the Holocaust. To this day my uncle David is a symbol for the Jewish people of Médanos and of Ein Hashlosha, a symbol of sacrifice for the State of Israel.

Other ancestors of mine from this maternal branch had more humble careers. Marcos Volpin, my great-grandmother's brother Mashe, was a trucker, and another of her brothers was a doorkeeper at a Jewish institution in La Plata.

On my mother's paternal side of the family, my grandfather Zelik Turkenich left his hometown Luninec, close to Pinsk, in Byelorussia, in 1923. He left for Argentina not long after Poland invaded the western area of Byelorussia, during the war between the recently established Soviet Union and Poland, which lasted from 1919–1921. His brother Roberto already lived in Argentina, having immigrated there from Luninec a few years before.

Zelik was 20 years old when he left Luninec. On his Polish passport it says that he was 17 when he got to Argentina. When he obtained his passport in Bialistok, Zelik lied about his age so he would not have to complete the mandatory military service in Poland, and so that he could leave the country without any problems. This was a common strategy by the Jews of Byelorussia, Ukraine and western Russia (which at that time had been invaded by Poland) to avoid being enlisted in the Polish army. Much later, in 1976, in Argentina, my friend's boyfriend's mother would use this same strategy to save her son from being enlisted in the military service so he could leave to Israel. To achieve this, this woman petitioned the Population Registrar of the Chaco Province to change her son's birth date back one year by presenting a sworn declaration that her son had been born in 1957 and not in 1958, since Argentines born in 1956 and 1957 had been exempt from completing military service by decree of the government.

At about the same time that Zelik left Luninec, some of the most famous activists of the Zionist movement and of the Israeli political movement migrated to Palestine from the Pinsk region. Some of these activists included Haim Weizman, the first president of Israel; Menahem Begin and Shimon Peres, the two Prime Ministers of the country; and the president of the World Jewish Congress, Nahum Goldman. During this time, the Jews of Pinsk were at risk because of the nationalist Polish soldiers who were both anti-Semitic and anti-communist and who, under order of the Polish government, murdered Jews who were accused of having communist pasts in Byelorussia, Ukraine and western Russia.

During his adolescence, Zelik's parents sent him to high school in Pinsk, since in Luninec there were limits imposed by the Czar of Russia on the number of places for Jewish students. Because of these restrictions, very few young Jews of Luninec could study in the schools of their native cities. Those like Zelik who could not find space in a high school in their own city did not have any other choice but to go to other places in Byelorussia to go to high school. In Pinsk, during and after the Bolshevik revolution, Zelik was a student and communist militant, but he was not a Zionist. When Zelik left Luninec, his parents, Naftuli Turkenich and Dina Gulman, and two of his sisters remained in their native city. The other two left Luninec shortly afterwards; Batsheva went to Israel while Rosa went to Argentina. Naftuli died of natural causes in 1939. In 1940, when the Nazis invaded Byelorussia, Zelik lost all contact with his mother and other two sisters.

We can only speculate as to what happened with his mother and one of his sisters. It is most likely that they were murdered by the Nazis during the invasion of Byelorussia during World War II (1939–1944). In August of 1941 most of the Jews of the Pinsk region were shot to death and buried in a mass grave.

The disappearance of my great-grandmother Dina and one of my aunts during the Holocaust is one of two personal connections with this sad period of Jewish history. My other connection is through Sonia, my wife. Raquel, Sonia's mother, spent a large portion of her adolescence in the concentration camp of Auschwitz and saw her entire family disappear.

Zelik's other sister, of the two that stayed in Europe, survived the war because she was able to escape to Russia before the Nazis came to Luninec. Towards the end of the 1970s when the Iron Curtain was opened slightly, many Russians left the Soviet Union for Israel. Amongst these Jews was Anatoli Golub, a son of this particular one of Zelik's sisters, who emigrated with his wife and son. Anatoli and his family emigrated around the same time that my family and I left for Israel, because of the military dictatorship of 1976 in Argentina. In a letter written in Russian, which my colleague Helena Doshlygina has translated to English, Anatoli Golub writes to my grandfather Zelik from Israel:

> We are finally in Israel. Mom wrote you a letter in which she briefly describes our life. We like being in Israel. The country is beautiful and rich. We are going to have problems finding jobs here because more musicians came to Israel than were needed. But that's not the most important thing, we can find different jobs. We are having problems with our son's studies. He studied the clarinet in the Soviet Union. Here they study it in a different way and he's going to have to learn again [...]. If your grandchildren are here in Israel we ask you to contact them. Maybe they can help us with our son's studies. This is very

important to us. Mom's sight isn't doing very well. She needs a magnifying glass to read and write. We impatiently wait for your response.

When Zelik first arrived in Argentina, he stayed in the city of Berisso, near La Plata, where his brother Roberto lived and he worked at the Swift meat packing plant until he retired, first as a worker and then as a foreman. He got this job through Doctor Mindlin, who worked as a doctor at the plant. Dr. Mindlin was the father of Lía Mindlin, Roberto's wife. Zelik and his wife Ana had two children: Annie (my mother), the eldest, was born in 1935 and Isaac, the youngest, was born about two years later. When Zelik retired from his job, he moved to La Plata where he founded Arañaluz, the biggest factory and retail store of lighting appliances in the city, located on 1st St. and 63rd St.

In La Plata he was an associate founder of the Max Nordau School and of the Keren Hayesod (the United Campaign to provide economic help to the State of Israel). During his long, healthy and active life, he participated in many cultural, political and religious activities in the Jewish community of La Plata, first at Max Nordau and then later in the AMIA. During the last years of his life he also occasionally acted as *hazan* (liturgical singer) in the celebrations of Rosh Hashanah (New Year) and Yom Kippur (Day of Atonement). Zelik served as the librarian of the AMIA Center until he passed away in 1990 at 87 years of age. His wife, my *bobe* (grandmother) Ana, died in 1992. In December of 2004 I visited his grave in the cemetery of La Plata where Zelik lies buried next to his wife Ana.

In a conversation (La Plata 11/14/03) with Amalia Miropolsky de Minoli, Zelik's niece, she remembers my grandfather:

EDF: What memories do you have of my grandfather Zelik?

  A: Your grandfather loved to go horseback riding; going fishing, for example, at the Ombusta farm because there was a lake there. He wasn't a farm man, but there he would be transformed, with the traditional cookouts and his facón [gaucho knife]. In Russia he was a communist and in La Plata he organized Max Nordau. During his vacations he would take trips to the countryside. When classes would end, your bobe would go to Médanos with the kids. Your grandfather would join them when he got vacations for a month/month and a half. He had a passion for working in the fields, working with the animals. Your grandfather Zelik and your grandmother Ana were married on the farm, in the barn, by zeide [grandfather] Volpin, at a party that lasted all night. Bobe Mashe did everything, not like today where all you have to do is go to a supermarket, while every morning your zeide would go with Marcos and Maike to the farm to work. He would get to the country and work. He would go to work at the farm in Médanos even though he was on vacation.

EDF: How did Zelik and Ana meet?

A: Your grandfather came to La Plata and ended up being a tenant of one of your grandmother's aunts, Aunt Malque. That's where the romance with Ana began [she was there visiting]. That's where they met. Her name was Malque Sterenchus.

The Paternal Family

I pity the poor immigrant
Who tramples through the mud
Who fills his mouth with laughing
And who builds his town with blood

–Bob Dylan, *I pity the poor immigrant*

Much like my great-great-grandparents on my mother's side, my paternal great-grandfather Marcos Faingold and my great-grandmother Neja Shein, left their small town of Besarabia (Moldavia, Romania) with their children and headed to Argentina in 1890. Those were the first years of European immigration to Argentina. Marcos Faingold and Neja Shein were among those who founded the Algarrobos Jewish colony, 15 kilometers from the town of Carlos Casares. This was also the property of the JCA of Baron Mauricio Hirsch and where sunflowers were first grown in the country. In 1890, my great-grandmother Neja gave birth to my grandfather Abraham Faingold on the boat headed to Argentina. Soon after arriving, Neja passed away and was buried in Algarrobos. She was the first person buried in the cemetery, one of the first Jewish cemeteries in Argentina.

Shortly after Neja Shein's death, Marcos Faingold got remarried to Berta Rosenbaum, Teper's widow. With her she brought her two children, Paulina (my future grandmother) and Israel. Paulina Teper, Enrique Faingold's mother, passed away when she was 38, when my father was only four years old. My great-grandfather Marcos (my grandfather Abraham's father

Exile From Argentina: A Jewish Family and the Military
Dictatorship (1976–1983), 2nd Edition, pages 9–14.

and my grandmother Paulina's stepfather) died only months after Paulina's death (so my aunt Teresa told me). My grandmother was cultured and a lover of literature. My grandfather Abraham passed away in 1966 of old age at my Aunt Teresa's home in Buenos Aires. According to Teresa, Enrique suffered greatly from his mother's death, not only because he was very young but also because he found out about it from a friend. During my father's childhood and adolescence, his sisters Natalia and Teresa, and to some extent his cousins Julita and Rosita—Israel Faingold's daughters—were like his adoptive mothers.

In the book *Colorados,* Hugo Fernández Faingold (Julita Faingold de Fernández Artucio's son) explains the origin of the last name Faingold that "must be of a Jewish-German origin [. . .]. My great-grandmother, who came from Russia to the colonies of Baron Hirsch, in Argentina, was married to a Mr. Teper, when my grandfather was born. Shortly thereafter my great-grandfather passes away. Then, the rabbi quickly marries her with an older man with the last name of Faingold, who shortly after adopts the Teper boy and changes his last name."

In summary, risking confusing the reader even further, my grandmother Paulina and her brother Israel, the children of Berta Rosenbaum (Teper's widow) went to live with great-grandfather Marcos when the children were very young. Marcos adopted Israel and years later married Paulina (my grandmother) to Abraham, one of his children from his first marriage to Neja Shein.

My great-grandfather Marcos did not do well in the farm in Algarrobos. So, the Faingolds left this colony, along with a group of families, and founded a town, which today is the city of Roberts, in the western area of the Province of Buenos Aires. In Roberts, the Faingolds dedicated themselves to the business and export of leather, general goods and, later, the making and selling of clothing.

In a conversation (Buenos Aires, 09/23/03) with my aunt Teresa Faingold of Korbenfeld, she tells me some facts about the history of the Faingold family:

> **EDF:** Where did your grandfather, my great-grandfather, Marcos Faingold come from?
>
> **T:** From Russia, where everybody came from. You know that Marcos Faingold died one month after mom did. We were young. He started banging his head against the wall; he got sick and died. My mother was his daughter-in-law, but he loved her like a daughter. The old Faingold got married to the Teper widow and their kids

began being born: uncle Gerardo, uncle José, uncle Samuel, aunt Ester, aunt Flora, Elena, Sarita, Paulina.

EDF: Was it your aunt Paulina who was married to one of General Ramírez's brothers?

T: She was one of Marcos Faingold's daughters. When she was very young she was given to another family. Grandpa said he couldn't raise her. I met him when I was young. She didn't want to have anything to do with her brothers or her family. She took her husband's last name, Ramírez, [Argentine President] General Ramírez's brother. She showed up here, in Roberts, when I was young. I met her. Her name was Paulina. She died, and her children are still here, but they don't associate with us. You know who they associate with? With Sarita and aunt Flora, but barely. I think her children didn't know the truth, [that their mother was Jewish]. She was a teacher, very well educated. They went to Entre Ríos to live so they wouldn't be close to her brothers. Her husband Ramírez wanted her to get in contact with her brothers. I was about 6 or 7 years old when he came to Roberts. I remember it as if it were today. My mom was still alive, and he said he wanted to unite the family, that they should get together and that he would figure something out so they would meet. They met in Carlos Casares, but she didn't care. She felt rejected because she was given away. "If he raised the others, why didn't he raise me too?" Dad came on a Sunday when they were going to meet at a hotel in Carlos Casares. Dad came back pissed off. Her husband wanted them to reunite, but she didn't. Not even with uncle Gerardo or uncle José. She was close to dad's age, and she was the youngest of them all. Dad said she was very pretty, that she came with the group that was given land in Algarrobos. In that group there was a married couple who had no children so they gave her to them to be raised. Later they went to Entre Ríos to the colonies there and she began working as a teacher. In those times it was an honor to work as a teacher. Your aunt Natalia called me and told me, "What do you think of this Teresa, we are part of the Republic's presidential family." But she didn't care and told us not to visit her or bother her anymore. Later they moved her to a school in Hurlingam as a principal of a school there. She didn't tell any of this to her friends. She has children from a military family, and she didn't want her children to know the truth. Her children were Jewish too, but not in her eyes. When Sarita passed away, I met one of her daughters. In other words I met one of my cousins, who looked just like aunt Rajel: identical. There was also a sister. Grandfather Faingold went around spreading children, in Canada: aunt Tsivie, my grandfather and grandmother's sister. When they came from Russia, my grandmother was pregnant with dad, who was born on the boat, a Rumanian boat, but they considered him Argentine. They sent Tsivie away, so as not to come with so many children, to Canada with an aunt. He told the aunt that they would come and get her in a year, but never did so.

EDF: Was your grandfather Marcos first married to my great-grand-mother, Neja Shein, with whom he came from Russia?

T: Yes, my dad's mom wasn't Grandmother Berta. Marcos Faingold and Neja Shein, and his second wife, Berta, came with my mother, her daughter Paulina, from another marriage. And Grandfather Marcos said that Paulina was for Abraham, my dad. You get the impression that my mom and dad were siblings, but they weren't. Everybody would ask, "How is it that siblings got married?" They were two widows with children. My dad's mother was pregnant on the boat, from the first marriage. Your dad, your brothers and I are all blood descendants from Neja Shein, my dad's mother, and from Berta Rosenbaum, my mom's mother. My dad and mom were raised together but had different mothers. Everybody in Roberts would say, "But you were married as siblings?" And it had to be explained to them, "They were two widows with children and a couple was formed with one child from each marriage." According to the Jewish religion, that is not a problem because they are not siblings.

EDF: Did they call you *Jew* in Roberts?

T: No, they would call us Russian. They would call my dad "The Russian." I remember when kids in school would say to me, "You're a Russian and your dad buys leather" and I thought that was shameful. I started crying and told the teacher. How she got that girl in trouble! Luckily, right?

EDF: Did your dad speak in Yiddish to you?

T: No.

Raquel Zimerman de Faingold, Israel Faingold's wife, shares in her *Memorias* that when her husband was a young boy he went to live at my great-grandfather Marcos Faingold's house, along with his mother Berta and his sister Paulina: "At that time a man named Faingold had been left a widow, his wife having died after giving birth. He had four children: Rajel, Abraham, Paulina and Syvie (who stayed in Russia). The family began to arrange the marriage of Faingold to Berta Rosenbaum. The marriage took place, and the family was left with four children, because one of Faingold's daughters was given to another family to be raised. When the two families joined through the marriage, the colony administration did not allow them to join their lands, so they could only keep one of them [...] My husband, Israel, had to stay in Teper's home until his mother went to get him [...]. Soon after Berta got pregnant and José was born [...] the marriage of Faingold - Berta Rosenbaum had ten more children: José, Miguel, Samuel, Gerardo, Isaac, Flora, Ester, Julia, Elena and Sara."

Raquel also tells that years later, in 1920, her mother-in-law Paulina (my grandmother) along with her husband Abraham (my grandfather) and their three children (my uncle Naúm, and my aunts Natalia and Teresa; my father had not been born yet) went to live with her and her husband Israel Faingold during a difficult period in my grandparents' life:

[A] letter from my mother-in-law Paulina, Israel's mother's and father's sister, arrived. It was a sad letter, tearful where she told that things were going badly. They didn't even have enough to eat. Israel and I did not know what to do. He thought they would come without even waiting for a reply. And so it was. They came before receiving a response with advice. We housed them in the tin house [that was at the back of our house], we had to build a very large room in our house and they came there to live with us [...]. [W]e lived in a very tight space, with only one bathroom [...]. It was a sacrifice, but we dealt with it.

Long after, in the early '40s, when Enrique was a teenager he found himself in a similar situation to that of his parents and brothers in 1920. At that time, because he was lacking economic means, he had to live at his aunt Raquel and uncle Israel's house for a while during his high school years in Buenos Aires. Enrique was treated like a son by his aunt and uncle and like a brother by his cousins Rosita and Julita. Both of them, especially Julita, encouraged and supported him to study and do something worthwhile with his life. In her *Memorias*, Raquel narrates,

During that time Israel managed to get a job as a salesman and things went quite well for him. Rosita worked at the store owned by the Kweller brothers. Julita got a job at an office of a textile factory [...]. We lived on 1654 Yerbal Street, and since the house was big, with a patio and a terrace, I had a lot of work to do: doing the laundry, ironing, cooking, and taking care of those who worked [...]. On Yerbal Street everything started looking better. Everybody was working and we were getting along very well [...]. [In] the year 1939 [...] things [were] no longer so easy [...]. My daughters were not earning as much. They were already ladies and had greater expenses.

In a conversation (Montevideo, 11/24/03) with Julita Faingold de Fernández Artucio, my dad's cousin, she tells me about the time when Enrique lived in her house:

EDF: Why did my dad go to live in your house when he was in high school?

J: It's that Enriquito, your dad, was very intelligent. We weren't that far apart in age, but I put him up to studying. He didn't want to go study at the Liceo, I remember that clearly. We would call him Enriquito. We weren't in a good financial situation. At that time I would go to Roberts to visit. I saw your dad behind the cash register at the liquor store that your grandfather owned. By then your grandfather Abraham had began selling leather. He was doing very well, but he began to have some family problems. What I remember of your dad is from when he was at my house in Buenos Aires. But I remember him as if the age gap between us was bigger, as if I was much older. I was only three years older than him. I have a blurry memory of your father when he was younger. Besides that there was the music he would make up. I asked him who had taught him. He would take a long comb and silk paper and he would produce beautiful sounds and who knows what other sorts of other kinds of art. He was very smart, but he didn't want to study. He would always listen to his older sisters; I think his brother Naúm didn't have a very big influence over him. Your dad didn't talk much. I told him, "Go to high school, you'll like it", for someone who can manage it easily. It was his first year of high school; I wasn't going to let him not attend. I knew that if he started he would enjoy it. He passed his first year very easily.

PART **2**

An Argentine Kid

In La Plata

Cuánto hace que no duermo nunca en paz
Esperando que ellos lleguen
A mi puerta a golpear
Porque desde que reinan las sombras
Reina el terror azul sobre la ciudad

–Claudio Gabis, *Blues del terror azul*

I was born in the city of La Plata on September 6, 1958. I am the son of Enrique Faingold and Annie Turkenich. My parents were married in 1956 and their first son, Roberto Luis, was born one year later. I, Eduardo Daniel, was born eleven months and twenty days after him; three years later Jorge Alberto was born and thirteen years later my sister, Paula Inés, was born.

Enrique, my dad, always worked as an engineer at the Ministry of Public Works (Ministerio de Obras Públicas) of the Province of Buenos Aires, where he got promoted to a high office. He also was a professor in the College of Science at the National University of La Plata. The publication *Quién es quién en La Plata* (Who's Who in La Plata) of 1972 informs us that Enrique Faingold

> studied in the College of Physics and Mathematics at the National University of La Plata (1952); [who] [s]ince 1956 has worked in the fields of Algebra, Calculus and Analytical Geometry in the School of Physics and Mathematics; [who] [h]as worked in various positions at the Ministry of Public Works and

at the Department of Public Sanitation; [who] is the chief engineer of the Department of Projects and Studies, in the section of Civil Works[;] [and who] [w]as sought out by the French government to continue a course on sanitation techniques during 1965–66.

Annie, my mom, got an Associate Degree from the College of Commerce and had begun to study Law at the National University of La Plata before she got married. After marriage, she stopped studying—as that was the common thing to do at the time—and dedicated her time to her family and to household work. Eventually, Annie began working in the administration section of my grandfather Zelik's factory and retail store of lighting appliances.

Roberto and I were less than a year apart, and as children we were inseparable. We would always be together playing Cowboys and Indians, playing on the swings, racing on our tricycles in the garden of our first house in City Bell or playing with a rubber ball in the backyards of our homes (first on 6th and 39th Street, and then on 6th and 61st). With my brother Jorge, who was three years younger than me, I didn't play as much, which could have been because of our age difference. We became closer when I came back home in 1979 to complete my military service. By that time he was already seventeen or eighteen years old. Paula was born when I was sixteen; during the few years that we were both at home I enjoyed watching her learn how to walk, talk, draw and, later on, watching her play with our cousin Danielito and talking to her friends on the phone.

When we turned ten or eleven, Roberto and I were no longer as close as we used to be. At that time he played soccer and was a very good swimmer. I wasn't very athletic; I preferred reading and collecting Batman and Superman comics, as well as drawing and painting. I always liked to think that I was my grandmother, *bobe*, Ana's favorite grandchild. *Bobe* Ana was like my soul-mate and I loved spending the weekends at her house eating and watching TV with her. Her breaded steak and the potato pie that she would prepare on Saturdays, and the homemade spinach raviolis with a veal stew on Sundays were out of this world.

When I was around twelve or thirteen I started collecting stamps and reading adventure books—especially books about the pirate Sandokán, *Tiger of Malaysia* by Emilio Salgari—and science fiction books by authors like Ray Bradbury, Clifford Simak, Isaac Asimov. At age fourteen I became interested in more serious books on history, literature and philosophy.

Roberto and I went to the same elementary schools: the Escuela Anexa and the Escuela Hebrea Bialik, and to the same high schools: the Liceo Víctor Mercante and the *tichon* (high school) of the Escuela Hebrea Bialik.

From ages nine to 18, both Roberto and I were members of the Zionist-socialist Ijud Habonim youth movement, an affiliate of MAPAI, a left-wing political party of Israel. My younger siblings went to different schools: Jorge went to the Escuela Anexa for part of his elementary schooling, spent part of high school years at the Bellas Artes, and then finished his studies at the Normal 3 school.

In 1972 I started high school at the Liceo V. Mercante in the 3rd division C. I graduated from high school in 1976. During my sophomore year of high school, I realized that I loved literature and studying history and philosophy on my own, almost as much as I hated going to school. During that time I started skipping school so I could go to the library at the National University of La Plata, which was close to my house, to read books, newspapers and magazines. I was especially interested in World War II, the Vietnam War, the American Civil War, the culture, music and politics of the '60s and Argentine and Latin-American history and literature. Almost every day I would read the newspaper *La Opinión*, published by Jacobo Timerman, the famous journalist who was kidnapped and tortured by the military during the dictatorship. I would also read the newspaper *El Día* and the *Gente* and *Siete Días* magazines, as well as the *Reader's Digest*, which my parents would buy on occasion.

Here I would like to include an interesting note: in October of 1976, about two months before the end of high school classes, my family and I were almost ready to leave the country. During that time my mom knew the principal of the school, Mireya Etcheverry, because she had been my mother's high school teacher years before. Thanks to her intervention, my teachers allowed me to take my exams early, allowing me to graduate from high school and leave Argentina with my diploma before classes were over.

A few months later, in the Gan Samuel kibbutz in Israel, I realized I had been very lucky to graduate from high school, having met a couple of kids from Córdoba who had had to leave the country in a hurry without being able to graduate. They had to finish high school at local schools in Israel, while I was able to begin the *mechina*, a preparatory school for the University of Jerusalem, immediately.

While I was at the Liceo, my views on politics were not very clear. I was somewhere between Zionist-socialism and Marxism which was more international than national. Besides the Ijud Habonim, I wasn't a member of a political party (and certainly not any armed political group), but I did have many political arguments with my classmates. This started when, in 1973, the General Assembly of the United Nations declared Zionism as racism. Because I was a Zionist, a classmate (we'll call her A) of the UES (a group of high school students who supported Perón) would call me a "traitor." She did this even though I attended the protest for student bus passes at the Ministry of Public Works where, ironically, my dad held a high position; this protest appears at the beginning of the film *La noche de los lápices* (Night of the Pencils).

I clearly remember A, someone who supposedly had progressive and left-wing revolutionary views, telling me that I was a lackey of Zionist imperialism, and that Zionism was an instrument of Yankee imperialism and colonialism. Her arguments always seemed to me to be rooted in anti-Semitism hiding under the cover of anti-Zionism. But at least during this time I could discuss politics without getting in trouble, be it with this classmate or with others of differing political views. I didn't talk at all with the fascists of the CNU and others in my high school class who belonged to the right-wing "nationalist" groups. Even today it is hard for me to think of them as "classmates."

In 1974 and '75, while dining at my grandparents' house on Sundays, Roberto and I would get into agitated political discussions with my grandfather Zelik, who had been a communist in Soviet Russia. We would take the line of Ichud Habonim of the 1970s, which defended the rights of Palestinians, believed they deserved their own state and should have their land, which was occupied by Israel during the Six Day War in 1967, returned to them. My grandfather Zelik had become a right-wing Zionist and follower of Likud, the Israeli party of Menahem Begin who had adopted the revisionist ideas of Zeev Jabotinsky. He not only rejected the idea of a Palestinian state, but also rejected the existence of the Palestinians in general. Thus, during that same time, I had my personal political disagreements with Zelik. I defended socialist ideas (Marx, Lenin, Ché Guevara, etc.). Zelik, meanwhile, was the owner of a factory who had workforce problems due to the new labor laws put in place by the Peronists and the grievances that his employees filed with the Ministry of Labor.

Of all my classmates, the ones that I remember most dearly are Armando and Mónica, a married couple who have two children. The three of us went to high school at the Liceo together, were part of the same group of friends and we would go out and study together. Today we are still close friends and we get together when I visit Argentina. Neither of them were members of political parties (which was almost the norm at the time) even though their ideas tended to be leftist. Now, Armando is an architect and Mónica is a lawyer.

In a conversation (La Plata, 09/05/03) with Armando and Mónica, they talk about the events that occurred in the 1970s and 1980s.

EDF: Did you go to the protest for the student bus passes?

  A: I don't remember going to the protest, but I remember the day when they were talking in school about going to the protest. Classes were cancelled so many times every month . . . In 1974 it was the bomb . . . the bomb with which classes ended. That year school ended early. In 1974 the Montos [Montoneros] were at the school.

  M: Maldonado interrupted school during our junior year and Mireya Etcheverry during our senior year. We didn't have a senior party, nor did we get our high school diplomas. Mireya had soldiers come to the school. Since they didn't let us have a party, our mothers organized a reception at the club Narciso and Goldmundo. We were very angry.

  A: We were already dating. By that time the Opus Dei gained control. Your brother Roberto had already graduated by that point too. What was he studying when the soldiers came to get him?

EDF: He was already in Israel.

  A: Oh, he was already in Israel. And you went to school the next day! That's crazy! They were misinformed.

  M: Actually, you were very lucky that they didn't take you, too. But, what was your brother's position?

EDF: He was the delegate of the division.

  M: For that?

  A: But nothing happened to your younger brother.

EDF: He was a child.

  M: Didn't they take babies? They would take children. Like the case of the Mercader family, the father was a judge and the son was a famous lawyer, they took them all; the wife, the children, him, his brother . . .

  A: They were very inconsistent. The only thing I remember was that this guy's brother, Carlitos' brother, took me to someone else's house and tried to get me to join the Communist Party. They gave me something to drink and they kept talking and talking, and I kept telling them 'no, no, no'. They wanted me to sign on, and they gave me a bunch of magazines. I left those in the bathroom at home, and among them was the affiliation card. And when my mom found them she had a panic attack. But I was 16. Not even 16, I was 15.

EDF: Do you remember the hall monitor that would say that you and I were subversives?

A: That was our senior year. It wasn't the monitor; it was the philosophy teacher, Rossi, the one that we always gave a hard time. I would mess with him because of what he would say about Christianity being dead as a philosophy. I would also tease and ask him, "but, why did it die?"

M: And one time they sent Marta and me to the principal's office.

EDF: How did that story end?

M: It ended the same way as Marta's story in which she insisted that life wasn't fun. The hall monitor called her in and told her that Rossi was saying that she and Faingold were subversives.

A: The hall monitor said that Rossi went to the principal's office and said that there were two subversives in the class. And he called the two of us in. Do you remember the little book we had to study? It had a red cover. The guy looked like a soldier, talked like a soldier.

M: At Bellas Artes they have a whole mural for the "Noche de los lápices" with all the student's names. If you go to Bellas Artes it's like being back to the '70s.

A: Bellas Artes was always more . . . The Liceo was always more politically reserved.

M: Do you remember when they killed a student? Who was found in a ditch, and we were in mourning all afternoon. We were crying all afternoon. A girl was found dead in a ditch, a very pretty girl. And when we went into the Carlos Estarita classroom with the flags! Remember that Carlos Estarita was a "monto" [Montonero] who was leaving when we were in our sophomore year; besides that he was a hall monitor and was found dead. When we got to school, this guy, Atili, showed up and started saying, "classmates, they killed the hall monitor, the last classroom on the first floor will be called Carlos Estarita."

M: And Elsita? Was she a Peronist?

A: Do you remember that we went to Elsita's house? It was for a meeting that I didn't understand. It was to create a group in our school class.

M: One time coming from Buenos Aires, it must've been in 1977 in the middle of the military dictatorship, we were going along the River Plate. They would stop buses everywhere. They made me get off the bus, and then the bus was leaving. They'd confused me with somebody else. It was in '77 or '78. The bus was leaving and the soldier was asking, "name of mother, father, where do you study, and why are you going out with him." Another one would come and it was the same thing all over again. I would cry and tell them, "I'm not who you think I am." It was only a few minutes, but I sometimes have nightmares about it. From a distance you realize that they took anyone. If they had doubts they would take you to a ditch and you would never be heard from again. The most famous one here was La Cacha. Now they're opening many places and taking groups of people to revisit the place where they were kidnapped and held, and they go with a therapist . . . it's terrible. And they remember, and there's blood there and things they had written on the wall. In Rosario there are also a lot of people who escaped.

EDF: How did you survive during the dictatorship?

  M: I was in college. We didn't have a lot of money, and didn't go out much. I remember that one time we went out with two other couples to eat, and the soldiers stopped us. We would study. We would stay at home. We wouldn't go out at night because we couldn't.

  A: After 1978 things changed a lot. I was in my first year of college when we had the World Cup. It was all new. I went to college during the dictatorship. I didn't know college any other way. When democracy was reinstated, I went back to the college as a lecturer. There were a few professors who had stayed and would talk about what the college had been like before the military dictatorship. Before the bombing in the Liceo happened, there had been a shooting in the College of Architecture, in the classrooms.

  M: We were already living through that in the Liceo. Don't forget that we already knew terror and repression with Perón's last government. When the triple A. . . that's when total chaos started. Do you remember when they asked us all for three passport photos? It was so they could identify us. The soldiers came into the school. A little soldier dressed in green said, "These are orders, you must bring three photos by tomorrow." We had to bring three passport pictures and give them to the soldier. Do you remember Lucila, our senior year history teacher, who gave us the advice to "wear sneakers so you can run"? I'll never forget that. We went to her house and she told us to wear sneakers so we could run from the soldiers. I remember that I didn't want to wear sneakers, but we had to. When we would enter the school, there would be a soldier on each side of the door. They had the pictures and they would look at you. My dad worked for ENTEL [the phone company] and told me not to say anything over the phone, "all the telephones are bugged, and they're listening to everything." They would take anyone. They would see you with some friend or some neighbor and that was it! We were so lucky that they didn't take us. We were very lucky. They would take anyone. It was on that trip to Córdoba, when we were hitchhiking and wearing those red ponchos... We went to La Rioja with a group of backpackers and I met this guy who was part of the ERP.

A: I met this one guy that was staying in the same hotel. When I got back here I phoned him and we went to Agustín Pereira Lucena's house, an Argentine guitarist who played Brazilian music spectacularly. He cracked the door open and told us, "Sorry guys, I'm leaving for Brazil, I'll be back in March" and shut the door.

M: We picked up those backpackers and that other guy and they were all part of the ERP.

EDF: Did they tell you this?

A: They were like everyone else, just talking bull.

Cecilia and Elsita were also classmates of mine at the V. Mercante School in La Plata. Today they are professors at the University of Buenos Aires. Cecilia was part of the same group of friends in high school, along with Armando, Mónica, Andrea, Graciela, Marta, Marisa and Sandra. Elsita had a different circle of friends. They were leftist followers of Perón. Cecilia was an active member of the "Third World Church", even though she came from a traditional Christian family of La Plata. Elsita, like her father, was dedicated to traditional Peronism. In 1976, at the age of seventeen, they both had to move to Buenos Aires. Cecilia's life had been threatened for working with the Third World Church, and paramilitary police officers had taken over Elsita's house in search of her father who was a sociology professor at the University of La Plata.

In a conversation (Buenos Aires, 10/24/2003) with Cecilia and Elsita, they talk about events of the 1970s and 1980s:

EDF: When did you leave La Plata?

C: I left in March of 1976. In July of 1975 my brother had an accident. I remember that we would count the bombs that exploded every night.

EDF: They also planted a bomb at [M]'s party, [L]'s sister.

E: I was at that party. We had already been chased out of La Plata. My dad was friends with [L] and [M]'s dad. Their dad was a fascist, my dad was a leftist. They were friends who could spend time together even though they had different ideas. We were already in Buenos Aires and we would always get on their nerves, insisting that we wanted to go back to La Plata. We were very upset about leaving La Plata. I would always be thinking of La Plata and I wasn't thinking about the dangers and risks.

C: I remember that I would always go visit [A], the pretty brunette from our class. She was the first one to leave, after her boyfriend "disappeared."

E: Juancho

C: We met up at the telephone office; I was trembling when I saw her.

E: When my dad came back from Venezuela we fled our house and we had the feeling that with the coup, things were going to be resolved. The thing is, we left La Plata because [L's dad] warned my dad that they were going to come for the "leftists." You can see how people were still loyal to friends regardless of everything that was going on. [L's dad] warns him and we leave. Within the first two weeks of April that party takes place. We wouldn't stop bothering them and annoying them about wanting to go back to La Plata, and we went. That's where there was an attack and one person was killed. My sister was hurt and I still have scars on my arm. They threw grenades in the garden. It was the party.

EDF: Who did it?

E: I don't know, but remember that there was a fight between the CNU and the Montos.

EDF: Did they discover who did it?

E: No.

EDF: Did you guys get it for being leftists?

E: Do you remember that other girl, María José? We were in the 5th C division of our class and she was in the 5th E. María José also leaves La Plata quickly. Her older brother was part of the Socialist Movement, I think they killed him. There was also the other María

José's brother; she was friends with Gabriela Gallo, the daughter of the dean of the university. Her brother was involved in some left-wing acts and had to leave. María José landed in Buenos Aires, since there were [military] zones in Buenos Aires. . .in Buenos Aires they didn't look for us. They went to my house in La Plata looking for my dad, but it was a different area. I saw María José in a protest for the "disappeared" and she was scared of talking to me because of that attack. It had come out in the newspaper that we had been there. There was a lot of fear and people were very suspicious about talking to others. I finished my last year of high school in Buenos Aires. Some stupid things happened. Some girl identified us as communists. At the Nacional Buenos Aires it wasn't the same. A conservative, Manigilia, went to that school and reported on everybody. . . I was about to go to that high school. They didn't let me enroll; they wouldn't let me in because I wore pants instead of a skirt. It's a good thing they didn't accept me.

EDF: How could you get along with people who were the polar opposites of you?

E: We both knew very well that we were different. I was very close friends to [L] but you could start to see that the differences were growing. I couldn't keep up the relationship. At first I couldn't maintain them with many people in La Plata.

EDF: Is there an ideological barrier?

E: Yes, exactly.

EDF: Do you think it's inevitable?

E: I think so. You can't talk about anything and everything. You have to limit yourself to subjects that won't create problems. You can talk about guys, stories, and your children.

C: That happened to me with relatives in La Plata. I couldn't handle it. We were enemies. Those were the people that went to the Cathedral with Monseñor Plaza. I disliked that, I disliked it strongly. I went to church simply for social reasons. I didn't have a mystical goal.

EDF: How did you feel when they killed Angelelli and the other "Third World" priests?

C: Terrible, a pain . . . I thought that I had a moderate position, that I had left-wing ideals, but that I was against armed struggle; we had a very strong discussion at school. I was against armed struggle and I thought that my position couldn't be objectionable to anyone. At school they would tease me about the armed struggle, "the only thing you want to do is go camping." I constructed a view against fanaticism, but things were happening very fast. My position was clearly a minority one. I had moral objections to the armed struggle; I had a problem with the kidnappings. Now, when they started to attack the Church . . . We weren't fanatics, we would sing the Peronist march; we would go to the slums. I practically started teaching in the slums when I was a kid. I became a more radical leftist at that time. There were people who had left-wing views but, from my point of view, didn't cause such a big social conflict as other left-wing groups did. But they swept them away; they swept all those parties away. They promoted one of the priests at my church and sent him to the middle of nowhere; they sent another one to a church in who knows where.

EDF: And when did you stop being an activist?

  C: In 1977 they displaced all the priests and they brought in a right-wing priest. I remember that the little girls and I would paint murals about social justice and so on. The priest would come and say," Don't get those walls dirty." So then I started saying that in the Middle Ages communication was done visually, with ingenuity . . . they threatened me—with death—so I had to leave. They started calling my phone anonymously. I remember that [A] was terrified and she would tell me, "if you go by my house and see a blanket on the balcony, you get out of there, you leave, you don't ring the doorbell, and you don't come looking for anything." I had to go to the other side of the park to see her house, to see if I could ring the doorbell. Even today I can't bring myself to walk on the sidewalk past a police station. Do you remember that at the police stations in La Plata they would sometimes kill someone because they had stepped on the sidewalk? It was all messed up. In 1977 everything got worse. You couldn't make a mistake because if you were distracted talking to a friend and you stepped on the sidewalk in front of a police station they could shoot you. It was also like exploring—a search—a type of solitude in La Plata. We lost all our frames of reference.

  E: I wouldn't have left La Plata. It wasn't part of my plans. I didn't want to leave the high school.

  C: I would never have imagined it. Nobody could foresee such horror. They blew us away. All that was left was a pile of rubble. You would go to school and there was no graduating class, maybe only two idiots. And you had this bunch of teachers who were just fossils.

E: Here at the UBA as well.

C: People who couldn't or didn't want to open their mouths about anything. Here I got together a group of survivors who would help each other. The first few years were very hard. I was alone, very alone. Good supportive people. The first two or three years were very hard, very lonely. I came to Buenos Aires in a very bad state, broken down, and I didn't know what I was looking for. My family was a very traditional family. They would always tell me that what was happening with the dictatorship, my parents, my friends, "must be for a reason", and that "it's very good." It all added up to my breakdown, so frightened, they wouldn't even let me go to the bathroom.

EDF: Did you go to the famous protest about the high school bus passes?

C: I went to the one that appears in the movie "La noche de los lápices", we all did. I remember it clearly, I was in the back. We were a lot younger; we were juniors in high school. That I was so defiant made me more secure and faithful to my ideas, including the "Peronist" tradition. I came to Buenos Aires and I began to actively participate in a cell of the resistance.

EDF: Are you talking about 1977?

C: I'm also talking about 1980.

EDF: In the middle of the dictatorship?

C: In the middle of the dictatorship. Because you know how it makes you feel? Guilty. Because all the people you loved were killed. Then you're left with a tremendous amount of guilt. You say, "there has to be some meaning to all this." I secretly went to resistance cell meetings during the whole time of the dictatorship. My first husband also worked in the cell where there were both left and right-wingers.

E: My husband was Trotskyite.

EDF: Your dad as well?

E: No, my dad was a Peronist, a traditional Peronist.

EDF: Did you have to burn your books during the dictatorship?

C: When they threatened me over the phone, I started a fire and burned all my books and records. I remember one that I bought now, by Viglietti.

E: When we moved to Buenos Aires the only book my dad threw away was Mao's Red Book. Here you could find Marx, Lenin, everything. He also threw away all the "Descamisado" magazines. Do you know how hard it is to find those magazines now-a-days?

C: There were also books that were confiscated because of their titles, like "Nobody writes to the Colonel."

E: They destroyed my dad's entire library when they came into my house. They took a Russian novel with them, and left heavier books behind. I have a friend that worked with the archives of the police of Buenos Aires with the forensic anthropology team. How they had the profiles constructed! The profiles were perfect, be it ERP or Montoneros. They had built a system for intelligence and spying.

In 1976, at the beginning of the last dictatorship, my family and I had to flee to Israel because they came into our house twice; first the army and then the secret police task force (Coordinación Federal). Before the home invasions, on a winter night in 1975, they had placed an explosive device on the door to our house. That night police experts came to our house to de-activate it, and luckily it didn't explode. We never found out who placed it there or why. At that time bombs were exploding every night, left and right. Both times that they came into our house they were looking for my brother Roberto, who at the time was in Israel participating in a program for Jewish volunteers of Ichud Habonim, at the Rosh Hanikra kibbutz.

It's not clear why they came looking for Roberto. It could have been that a monitor of the Liceo, member of the CNU (a nationalistic, anti-Semitic, radical right-wing Catholic group), had filed a complaint and turned him in. My brother had gotten into a few fights with the monitors because of their anti-Semitic views or, maybe, they had picked him out since he had been the delegate for his division in the student assembly during the protest for the high school bus passes. This is like a scene at the beginning of the movie "La noche de los lápices." At the student assemblies most of the delegates were Peronists, but there were also a lot of communists and a minority were socialist delegates, radical and independent like Roberto. Another possibil-ity is that a classmate, kidnapped by the death squads, gave his name while being tortured, knowing that my brother was already out of the country. Re-gardless, Roberto was what the militars would call a "perejil," or parsley, a person whose life was worthless (at that time they were giving away parsley for free at the supermarkets).

We were very lucky that during the raids on our house they didn't take any of my siblings, parents or even me. In the first raid, a military squadron came to our house. I remember that uniformed soldiers kicked down our door and stole a valuable Omega watch that belonged to my father. One of the soldiers told my dad, "Sir, I apologize that we kicked down your door, it's just that sometimes they will shoot at us from inside." When I heard the screaming and I saw the soldiers breaking the door, as if by instinct I quickly removed the grill on the heater and threw in the four books that I had on my nightstand, which I still remember today: *Las Venas abiertas de América Latina* by the famous Uruguayan author Eduardo Galeano, *Principios elementales y fundamentales de filosofía* by the Marxist philosopher Georges Politzer, and *La muerte de familia* and *Nudos* by the anti-psychiatrists David Cooper and R.D. Laing. They were books that I would continuously study and would also use for the *peulot* (activities) of dialectic materialism that I gave the 12 and 13 year olds in the *ken* (nest) of the Ijud Habonim of La Plata.

The second home invasion, when a big group of the Coordinación Federal came dressed in civilian clothes and masked faces, was much more traumatic. I remember it as if it were yesterday. I was leaning against the dresser in my bedroom, on the second floor of our house, in boxers and a soldier with his face masked was slapping and hitting me in the face with a pistol, while another one asked me repeatedly, "Where is your brother Roberto?" "Are you religious?" and other questions I no longer remember. At the same time, from the corner of my eye, I could see that they had my father face down on the floor on the lower level of the house with a gun to his head, and a man with graying hair, wearing a brown overcoat, and another man with a masked face were talking to him. While all of this was going on, they had locked my mother and my younger sister in my parents' room on the second floor.

We were very lucky that before the second raid my dad had burned most of my books (without consulting me) that might have indicated that there was someone with left-wing views living in the house. At the time I didn't appreciate my father's cleverness for burning the books, and I remember that I had been very mad about it. Out of either fear or instinct, my dad had done the right thing. You could have found many different kinds of books in my collection: Marx, Engels, Trotsky, Fanon, Che, Mao, Neruda, and Benedetti. . . If the soldiers or the goons from the Coordinación Federal had seen them, I would probably not be alive to tell this story today. It was the home invasions, the burning of books, the bomb, the soldiers and right wing militias in the streets and in the schools and the fear. It was a very traumatic time period. Just like thousands of Argentines, after the military dictatorship of 1976, our family had no other option but to leave the country.

In a conversation (La Plata, 10/14/03) with Annie Turkenich de Faingold, my mother, she recalls what happened to my family during the '70s:

EDF: Do you remember the raids on our home from that time?

A: That night you came home in the early evening and told us, "the city is going to be a mess tonight, they just kidnapped Colonel Pita. There's going to be trouble . . ." It was you coming in from the street because you had found out that that night there were going to be raids on homes. It was the 30th or 31st of March. And the other one was on the 12th or 13th of August. I don't remember if it was the night of the 12th to the 13th or from the 13th to the 14th. And we immediately went to the Sochnut [Jewish Agency]. That night we all stayed together like baby chicks. The next day we went to get our passport pictures taken and to see the shaliach [Jewish Agency envoy] who was actually Enrique's cousin. It was during the second raid that I panicked the most. During the first one I yelled at them from upstairs, "but he's in Israel, he's in Israel." They were wearing uniforms and all. Then there was a girl who was in a military truck and who months later met Roberto in Israel and told him: "your mom was yelling at them from upstairs: but he's in Israel, he's in Israel." It was the uniformed army who closed off the street with the truck. I never knew who the girl was. I never knew her name or who she was.

EDF: Was this the first home invasion?

A: Yes, the first one came out all right, with the army with uniforms and all. The second one involved guys in all black with ski masks. Their faces were blackened so they couldn't be recognized. That wasn't the army; that was something else. Uniformed military men stole your dad's watch from his nightstand and made a mess of my house, they took out all the drawers. It was a lot of work to clean up the next day! But that was the army. They didn't find anything. They didn't find Roberto so they left. I was so traumatized that every night I would put Roberto's letters on top of the television set. Unconsciously, I waited for them to come back, everybody told me that wouldn't happen, but I had a feeling that they might return. On the 12th or 13th of August they ripped out the phones so nobody could communicate. These were the guys dressed in black, with the ski masks and blackened faces. There was also a guy in an overcoat who must have been a high official of some sort, wearing a hat. I saw him briefly before they sent me to my room with Paula who was three then. I was in the room with Paula and these guys were talking to you. These were the bad guys, not the army guys. It was the other ones, the second ones, who asked you, "are you religious?" They were looking at the pictures of the bar mitzvas. When they left it was around 4 or 5 in the morning, you all came to sleep in the big bed where we all lay together, terrorized, and I told your father, "we are leaving." And your dad said, "All right, as you wish." Your dad talked to the person of the Sochnut, who turned out to be a cousin of his that had come as a shaliach. Dad told him what had happened and the shaliach said, "but they didn't find who they were looking for. Israel is hard, you don't know everything." Then dad told him, "I'm going to ask for a leave permit for one year without pay, but keeping my job." We waited until six in the morning and your dad very fearfully got out of the car and we went to my mom's house, on 1st and 63rd streets. We rang the doorbell and told them. We went to the photography place on 1st and 60th.

EDF: We didn't have passports?

A: No. What passports? Had we ever traveled anywhere? The passport was so Roberto could go to Israel sometime and then everyone would study here. We had never seen Israel, we'd never been there. Mom and dad had, but not us.

EDF: Do you remember when they planted the bomb at our house in 1975?

A: Yes. A specialized explosives team from the police came. They took a long time getting there. We went to Waingortín's house to call them. We were coming back from the movie theater. You were sleeping. We stayed at the front door because we saw this pipe. Then a police officer that was going by stopped and told us, "stay on the sidewalk across the street, and don't go in." And some policemen went up and got you guys down and you came with us to our neighbor's gate across the street. We stayed there until the specialized team came in their little truck. Roberto was still there. It must have been winter time, in June or July. I remember that because I was wearing a fur coat. Roberto left on the December 26th. I remember because it was the same day that Rojele, your classmate from the schule [Hebrew School], passed away. It was the same time when they planted the bomb at the Chilean's house, the actor who lived a block away [Lautaro Murúa]; his son was Jorge's friend. Our windows shook from the explosion. Your dad had to open the front gate there; we were scared. The policemen asked, "Are there children?" I told them there were. They said, "Then we're going to get them out." It was pure chance that Roberto was coming back from the movies, or an outing, and you two were at home, and Paula at my mom's house. Roberto, who was just coming back, came over to us on the sidewalk. We had no idea! We didn't even realize it! They tell me things now, because people talk now; before one didn't talk about these things. I recently told our neighbors everything that happened to us. It was only recently that I told everyone. One felt like...but my best friend would tell me, "it must have been for a reason" [por algo será]. Later on my best friend wrote to me in Israel, "order has finally arrived here and we moved on to normality." All this while I'm living in a cramped little room in the merkaz klita [residence for immigrants], after living in a mansion. And we tried to make do when there wasn't any money to fill up the fridge, because the only money we had was from the sale of the car and we wanted that like it was made of gold. When everyone had sold their houses [and] had prepared to move to Israel, there we were. We were unprepared! That was an escape. We didn't even know what Israel was like; we didn't know what the climate would be like. I was so ridiculous! Do you know what I put in the suitcases? I put my fur coat. Where was I going to go? To the Israeli climate with my Argentine fur coat? I also took my party clothes, because I liked going to parties, we had groups of friends and we would go to the movies every Saturday. If there were parties one had clothes for them: long dresses and expensive shoes. Bobe [grandmother] and zeide [grandfather] had gone to Israel and they had brought me back an expensive fur coat. Those were times when they were very well off and they brought me back the furs which I still wear and will wear in Norway for Sabina's bat mitzva. Crocodile purse and shoes for Israel!

EDF: Were you scared of being raided once again when you came back from Israel?

A: No, we were so oblivious. I came back suffering from a deep, deep depression which left me in bed on medications because we didn't have a house anymore. We got back on September 11th; we came back from Ezeiza in the afternoon and all of our friends showed up at mom's house. I didn't have a house. Everybody asked us why we came back. I told them, "well, we couldn't adjust, Enrique didn't find a suitable job, the kids are fine, and they're studying." And Enrique went back to work, and we said, "We are going to try to sell the house", which was a white elephant. We were selling it cheap, but no one wanted to buy it. It was too expensive, too big. But oh well, we came back and Jorge came back in December and had missed the enrollment date for the Bellas Artes school. Your dad went to see Gallo, the dean of the university whom he knew from being on a scholarship trip to France together, so Jorge could continue his studies at the Bellas Artes. He told him that it was impossible because Jorge didn't have the prerequisites for music. Jorge was so mad! I noticed that he was mad about everything, but with such tenacity. We got back on September 11th and by the 12th Jorge was preparing to graduate from high school in December, and I was in the back room, lying in bed, taking medication day and night. I had a doctor who gave me lots of antidepressants. One pill, another pill, and I spent the entire day sleeping. I was depressed until we bought this apartment. One of the people who came to see the house was building these apartments on 8th and 48th Street. She was thrilled about the house and they gave us the apartment along with 3,000 pesos. It turns out that to return to Argentina, we had to return all the money the Sochnut had given us, including the plane fares and the ten months at the merkaz klita [residence for immigrants]. Everything was paid; it was a lot of money. My dad got a loan from the Banco Cooperativo, with warranties. They didn't give us anything. It was a lot of money for the surety bond, and the house would not sell. They sent us the money in Israel with a friend of theirs so we could leave. Enrique used to say that we were like prisoners in the merkaz klita, in that little room, number 202.

EDF: What do you remember about Paula?

A: For Paula it was wonderful because she turned four in kindergarten at the merkaz klita and she loved it. She had a wonderful morá [teacher] and she had Russian and Rumanian friends. We celebrated her fourth birthday at the kindergarten. All the kids came with presents. The ones who didn't have any money would draw pictures, and there's still a notebook and a drawing of two stick figures that a little Rumanian friend had given her.

EDF: How did Paula find things when you came back?

A: Paula started schule [Hebrew School]. She didn't notice anything different. She was with her best friend Paula Rosenfeld, whom she was still close to.

EDF: Did Paula have any traumatic memories of the home invasions?

A: She says that she doesn't remember any of it. She was really young, three and a half maybe four. It really affected me. It didn't affect your dad either. He says that he is an optimist. It was partly because Teresa was encouraging him to come back, that nothing happened.

EDF: What were they saying about those who "disappeared" when you came back?

A: I remember at that time that Timerman would go to the Hebrew University in Jerusalem to give lectures about the concentration camps. And I would say, "But this guy is poisoning your minds. We live here in Argentina, what concentration camps is he talking about?" Just look at how the situation went. Enrique came back without any work related problems and they even promoted him. Enrique didn't tell everyone the truth, but he did tell Cosak. And Cosak told him that someone from work who was very close to him had had many problems. One daughter ended up in Sweden. If she was Montonera or what, I don't know. In Sweden she married a Swede, but that marriage didn't last. You don't know how expensive it was for her father to bring her back with her son! Who knows how much money it cost? Enrique worked with the father right next to him and he didn't know about it. It wasn't common knowledge. I told the neighbors that we were going to Buenos Aires when they were packing our furniture to go to Israel. An old man walked by and asked, "Are you moving? But you just moved in!" Whether they knew or not, I don't know. Because that day the street was blocked off and the telephone lines were ripped out. "And how do we contact them now?" We had an acquaintance who was an electrician who would buy from zeide. So then we called him and told him that the girl had ripped out the telephone lines. She was playing and we got distracted and she pulled out the telephones, and he believed it. You know that I called him a year ago because I needed some work done and I then told him, "Do you remember, Ángel, when I called?" He said, "What a nice house you had!" I asked him, "Do you remember when I called you because the telephones were ripped out?" He said, "oy, those were rough times!" And it was passed off as if the girl had been the one who ripped out the phones, that's why the ones who came the second time were evil, not like the army.

My sister Paula was between two and three years old when the tragic events which forced my family to leave Argentina took place. At age four she returned from Israel with my parents. About twenty years later, when she was close to graduating with a major in English from the National University of La Plata, she decided to return to Israel. In La Plata she almost graduated with a degree in English. Today, Paula teaches Spanish at the Cervantes Institute in Tel-Aviv as well as teaching private lessons; she studies art at the Beit Berl Institute, close to Kfar Sava, and lives in Hod Hasharon with her husband Amir, an Israeli man, and their two children Liam and Noam.

In a conversation (Hod Hasharon, Israel, 05/11/04) with my sister Paula, she remembers what happened to our family in the late 1970s:

EDF: What do you remember from when you were in Israel?

P: I remember the merkaz klita. I remember that I would tell mom, "Mommy, don't cry, don't cry. Why are you always crying? Stop crying." But I don't remember much, it's very blurry. The first thing that came up was that I would say, "Mommy, don't cry, don't cry." I remember that they celebrated my birthday at the merkaz klita. I remember I had a Mexican friend who had bangs. I used to speak perfect Hebrew, with the accent grr, grr, grr. Today I'm kind of in-between, not just like an Argentine who got here yesterday.

EDF: Do you think the move to Israel affected you at all?

P: No, we were only there for eleven months . . . I was four years old.

EDF: Do you have any memories of the home invasions?

P: I only have a few images. I remember people on roofs carrying guns. I have images. I don't know if they told me about them or if I saw them, of rifles. I think I saw it, but I'm not sure . . . about the cars. Maybe it's from movies, like "La noche de los lápices."

Meanwhile, in Buenos Aires

> *Somos territorio de violencia*
> *Mi pueblo habla, mi pueblo grita*
> *Basta de muerte, basta*
> *Basta de morir, morir, morir*
>
> —Piero, *Que se vayan ellos*

Before I start telling of my own experiences outside of Argentina and in the Argentine Navy, I would like to relate some conversations that I had with my aunt Teresa Faingold de Korbenfeld and with one of my father's cousins, Rosita Faingold de Villagra, who witnessed the suffering of family members that occurred as a consequence of the military dictatorship. Both of them give the reader the chance to know what happened in Argentina in regards to the state terrorism caused by the military and paramilitary groups before the return of General Perón, during the government of Isabel Perón, and during the military dictatorship of General Videla in the '70s. Amongst these relatives we find the leftist senator and lawyer Rodolfo Ortega Peña, murdered by the triple A in 1974; Agustín Villagra, one of the historic founders of the FAR, killed by the Córdoba police as they attempted to kidnap an executive of the automotive industry of that city along with the help of his friend Carlos Olmedo, another of the historic founders of the FAR; Alberto Villagra, the founder of the socialist party in Tucumán and lawyer for leftist militants; Eduardo Galeano, famous Uruguayan author, author of *The open veins of Latin America*; and Mario Mactas, a journalist for

Exile From Argentina: A Jewish Family and the Military
Dictatorship (1976–1983), 2nd Edition, pages 37–44.
Copyright © 2024 by Information Age Publishing
www.infoagepub.com

important magazines like *Satiricón* and *Humor*. More details of the lives, and in some cases violent death, of these relatives are presented in *La voluntad* by Anguita and Caparrós and in other bibliographic sources which appear at the end of the book.

In a conversation (Buenos Aires, 9/23/03), my aunt Teresa Faingold de Korbenfeld speaks of Rodolfo Ortega Peña:

> **EDF:** Did you know Rodolfo Ortega Peña?
>
> **T:** Yes, through Elenita Villagra. They lived together. Elenita was with him when he was shot to death in downtown Buenos Aires; they were in a cab going to dinner. I was at the wake. I knew him because he was invited to a barbeque and he went with Elenita. Ortega Peña was an important man, very charming; it was very nice to hear him speak. That morning Rosita Villagra telephoned me: "Teresita, this and this and this has happened." How could I not go? And she was giving me directions, and there were police officers everywhere. There was a flight of stairs and a first floor. Everything was so gloomy that it was imposing, and there were no flowers. It wasn't ostentatious, just a sign. I didn't go to the cemetery, I think they wanted to go past the congress, but I went home. There were a lot of people, but a lot of people were scared.

In another conversation (Buenos Aires, 10/30/03) Rosita Faingold de Villagra, my father's cousin, talks to me about her relatives, including some notable political militants and intellectuals such as Agustín Villagra, Rodolfo Ortega Peña, Eduardo Galeano and others:

> **EDF:** Tell me about your husband.
>
> **R:** Alberto was the secretary of the Socialist Party in Tucumán, which was strong at that time. Alberto was the black sheep of the family. How did I meet him? Natalio, my brother, was studying engineering in Tucumán. They had taken over the university. I went to Tucumán to see Natalio and because we had a lot of relatives from my mother's side, there were about fifteen Zimermans there. One day we were taking a bus that Alberto and Carlos Santalla, who was the best man at my wedding, and Nicolás Repetto were riding. Nicolás Repetto was married to one of the Cherkovsky sisters, one of the older sisters. The other was married to the socialist representative Enrique Dikmann. We were traveling to Villa Nugués and Alberto and his friends invited us to join their table.

Carlos Santalla was making jokes, he had a great sense of humor; Alberto was the serious one. When we got to my aunt Ite and her husband Gabriel's house, my brother Natalio was waiting for us to take us sight seeing in Tucumán. I told him, "Listen, I met this guy Alberto Villagra." He told me, "He's one of our lawyers, he defended us." Alberto defended imprisoned students. One day they pick him up at a concert and take him to the police station, to the basement. The lawyers were able to get him out and he leaves to Buenos Aires for some time. He then went back to Tucumán and continued to be an activist for the socialist party. Then we got married on the 22nd of May in 1944. He went to Buenos Aires with his mother. He said that his mother was more of a socialist than he was; they were a whole clan. They didn't go to church. When he was a candidate, there were five Villagras at the table and three votes. He would say, "Who didn't vote for me?" I learned a lot about politics from him. Then Alberto traveled to Uruguay, where all the exiles were. We got married in May and in the month of October he sent me on a diplomatic mission to Uruguay to take Repetto's documents to him, who, at the time was exiled at Frugoni's house. Carlos Santalla was from Uruguay and he accompanied us along with my sister Julia. We got to Uruguay intending to find Repetto, who wouldn't give out his address because they wanted to kill him, to get him all these things. You had to talk to Hugo Fernández Artucio who was in charge of the Free World magazine which was closed because he wrote about the Nazi spies in Uruguay. Hugo Fernández Artucio was going to give us Repetto's address, but we spoke on the phone all the time and they wouldn't tell us where to find him. We finally found him on our own and gave him the papers. Repetto lived so humbly, but was in exile. When we got back to the hotel there was a message from Fernández Artucio telling us to meet him at a certain time at his studio and we should go with Julia, a beautiful single girl. When we open the elevator and we rang the doorbell, we started to crack up, "So why did we come here? What we had to do was already done!" We doubled over with laughter and at that moment he, who was a solemn professor, opened the door. I told him, "We came, but what we had to do has been done." He spoke to me but kept his eyes on Julia. He invited us to a party of the Victory Junta for the war [World War II]. We went with him. He would ask Julia to dance and she had no idea what to do. A few days later he came to Buenos Aires, even though he couldn't get into Buenos Aires, since everything was under immense control. Fernández Artucio came following her; he told mom and dad that he wanted to marry Julia. Keep in mind that he'd only known her for three days. They met in August and got married in October. I got married in May; in August he sent me on that diplomatic mission. They went to Uruguay to get married. My parents suffered, but they weren't against the marriage. They went with some women so that they could see that everything was alright. Fernández Artucio continued to fight for everything that he was fighting before, but he couldn't come to Buenos Aires. For my mom to visit her grandchildren she had to fly through Brazil to get to Uruguay. For every grandchild that was born in Uruguay she had to travel to Brazil and then down to Montevideo. She couldn't get there directly. When we got through with the Free World magazine, which had the Statue of Liberty on the back, they thought it was a fashion magazine. Julia stayed in Uruguay; he was a professor and dean of an institute between high school and university.

EDF: Tell me more about your husband.

R: Alberto continued to be a socialist activist in Tucumán. He was running for governor. I have a picture of the Casa del Pueblo. At that time the socialist movement was appealing and they had the town house that they had sacrificed to buy. My mother-in-law was scared to death because we had papers here and they had blacklisted him. . . he was on the list of people they were going to kill for being bad Argentines. The women cried so much! Things were very rough in Tucumán. Alberto continued to be an activist. In 1952 he decided to come to Buenos Aires to fight. That same year my third daughter Raquelita was born, and Eva Perón died. I have four daughters; the youngest one was born here. He was in the CELS, he was a part of everything, and he never hid it. He received a medal for being in the party for fifty years. As my brother-in-law [Eduardo Galeano] says, "few people are as perseverant as your husband." My daughter Liliana was not an activist, she was a doctor and they had killed some of her coworkers from the hospital. She was dating an Italian boy whose mother lived in France and she went there with him. She completed her psychiatry residency in France; she lived there for almost ten years. This is my second daughter, and Helena.

EDF: How is it that there are so many famous people in your family?

R: It started with the Berger girl, she was Agustincito's, my nephew's, girlfriend; he was Agustín Villagra's son, almost Alberto's twin. Do you remember the movie "Missing?" Agustincito Villagra's father was like the character of the father in that movie, the one who'd say "I wonder what he's up to?" He would say all the same things that fathers do when they are worried about their children. You have no idea what we went through! My brother-in-law [Eduardo Galeano] was exiled in Brazil and the Cóndor group would always go through and read his mail. Here, they would raid our homes; they would go through baby's cribs and pick them up just to see if there were weapons in the cribs. I don't know how we're alive after all those raids, it's a miracle.

EDF: Were your daughter Helena and Galeano the first to leave for Brazil?

R: Yes, that's where the famous journalist Eric Nepomuseno was; we lived at his house when we went to take our girl there. Helena left with Eduardo the day that they killed Santucho. Eric Nepomuseno came to get Helena. We took Marianita [daughter of Helena and the journalist Mario Mactas], who was very young. We took her to our house in the mountains, in San Luis. The day that Nepomuseno came to get Helena, there was a line of soldiers that were watching the people going by. We were in the mountains in San Luis and they had to let us know that they had gotten through. They left us a message on the telephone saying something like, "we got the package here." Helena made it there. The military knew about us because Rodolfo Ortega Peña had lived in our house in San Luis; he would practice shooting his gun in the jungle. We got ourselves involved in everything!

EDF: Tell me about your daughter Helena.

R: When Liliana left, the ordeal with Rodolfo Ortega Peña had already happened. Helenita suffered because she missed her family so much, our whole family is tightly knit. When Helenita was in exile in Brazil we took her little daughter Marianita. They had left Marianita with us. We spent a few beautiful days in Rio with the six year old girl. The next morning Mario called me and he brought the girl to me with a suitcase full of beautiful clothing. The next day when we went to the park we could see police officers watching us closely; that day I got a call at nine to tell me that Mario had been kidnapped. They told me, "We need to send Mariana to stay with you because they've kidnapped Mario." And I was asking myself, "Who is going to give me permission to send Mariana to Madrid with Helena and Eduardo?" Helena called me to see how the girl was doing and I told her, "They've kidnapped Mario." She fell silent. A friend said that he was kidnapped "because of his morals and habits." That's when they could breathe again; it wasn't because of Helena. I went to buy a plane ticket to send Marianita to Spain and my daughter Liliana's boyfriend, Pablo, came with me. They were going to Spain to get married because so many people they knew had been killed. I had to ask Mario to go and sign the papers so that Marianita could go to Spain as soon as possible because it was very dangerous for her. They had already tried to kidnap her once. Mario signed the papers at his lawyer's office and said, "They've given me forty-eight hours to leave the country." So Mario went to Colombia. Marianita travels with my daughter Liliana who is on her way to Paris to find her boyfriend Pablo.

EDF: How did you get to know of the prisoners of Trelew?

R: The Berger girl's father went to see Alberto at his studio because she was our nephew Agustín's girlfriend. This Berger girl had a big impact on Alberto; that's when he started working for the CELS. He was very involved with Trelew as well as in the López Rega times. They broke out of jail and a soldier helped them out; some were able to escape to Chile; Santucho was among them. This made a big impact on Alberto. Antonia Berger was our future niece; she was part of the FAR, on Alberto's side. Something worse happened with Chono, Neldita Villagra, Agustín's sister, who now lives in Switzerland. They were looking for Agustín's brother. They were in Córdoba. They were waiting for someone. There were three people there that we cared a lot about, not only Agustin-cito who I raised. He was two years old when I got married and he passed away when he was 29. That was terrible, it was terrible. They were looking for the two of them. When this incident hap-pened to Agustincito, his sister fled to Chile. Chono was staying with my family in Mendoza. Luz, Natalio's [Rosita's brother's] wife, got her a wig and a pair of glasses so she could cross the border; the police were even looking for them in helicopters. She man-aged to get her on a bus that went across the mountains. She got to Chile where Allende was; that's when they killed Agustincito. She also stayed at my mother's house and Liliana was with her. Her mother sent word that they had moved. This meant that they had raided their house in Tucumán. Agustín was so kind, so sweet; they have written poems for him, he was a wonderful boy. Both she and Agustincito were activists. Their mother, like your mother, suffered a lot. She went to work with Allende, with their group of activists from the '70s; she was a socialist. It was beautiful. Her mother went to see her, but she was on a visit to the mines. Her mother was always waiting for her to come back so she could be with her daughter. When they killed Agustín, his mother wasn't there; I had to go pick her up at the airport. I had sent her a telegram, "Agustín hurt. Come back." He was already dead in Córdoba. Helena was the one who had to go and identify the body. Helena was so young; she was in very bad shape after that. Alberto and Agustín [Agustincito's father] were like two old men who didn't know what to do. Alberto had completed all the legal paperwork to retrieve the body. Helena put herself in charge of identifying the body for her father and uncle's sakes. Facing her son who had 24 bullets in his body! It was terrible. Helena had to go inside to identify the body. She was just a young girl of 21 who was already married to Mario Mactas; Mariana had already been born. Mariana was born in 1970. They killed Agustincito in 1971.

EDF: What schools did your daughters attend?

R: Lily and Raquel went to the Nacional Buenos Aires. The other two went to other schools, but I don't think it's the schools you attend that makes you who you are. Helena and Elsita are very intelligent and well read even though they didn't go to the Nacional Buenos Aires. At my house we would always talk a lot at the dinner table. Liliana was a classmate of Carlos Olmedo, whom they killed the same time they killed Agustincito. Chono lives for her children and look what happened. I needed to go get her at the airport and tell her that Agustincito is dead; I had to break the bad news during the car ride. That was something terrible. I told her that Agustincito died for his ideals. I didn't know what to say to her when she had a nervous breakdown. She then joined the group of the Mothers of Plaza de Mayo with her friends and acquaintances that had been detained or had disappeared for some time. The Mothers say that their children gave birth to them. Chono, Agustincito's sister, was in Chile and she didn't dare come back. You should see how controlled that wake was; not many people dared show up. The cemetery was full of policemen dressed in civilian clothing; they were watching the people and taking photographs. Things were getting really ugly.

EDF: Like what happened with Trelew?

R: This had never happened before, shooting people down without a trial. Antonia was lying on the ground, pretending to be dead from a bullet in her head when a doctor comes along and realizes that she is alive. This is something you never forget. She was taken to the hospital and kept there under arrest, being watched. Alberto went to visit her at the hospital. He took with him the doctor that had saved my daughter Elsa from an accident on the street. This doctor, Dr. Muller, didn't want to help when he saw the situation. All of a sudden he said "no" and then didn't want to deal with the situation anymore; he was mad. Later Antonia was released, but was soon murdered. When the incident with Allende took place, my niece came back from Chile. She fell in love with one of the activists and married this man by the name of Lebensohn, who had a terrible asthma case. He was an FAR activist. He married Chono, deeply in love, and they moved to a small apartment where he continued to be an activist. He came to Buenos Aires and it seems that he had an altercation with those same activists. They say that he went into cardiac arrest at the time of his fight with his fellow activists. One time I was on a train with him and he started clutching himself because he was falling over from an asthma attack. His father was a famous author. His father's wife was killed. We went to where Lebensohn was staying in Ramos Mejía, and there he was: they were burying him. Chono wept and wept. She was destroyed.

In Israel

I got a baby's brain and an old man's heart
Took eighteen years to get this far
Don't always know what I'm talkin' about
Feels like I'm livin' in the middle of doubt
Because I'm eighteen I get confused every day
Eighteen I just don't know what to say
Eighteen I gotta get away

—Alice Cooper, *I'm eighteen*

In the beginning of November 1976, my parents, my siblings and I arrived to Israel with the help of the Jewish Agency. At that point all the members of my family all went to different cities: my parents and my sister went to the *merkaz klita* (immigrants residence) in Haifa, Jorge was in another *maon* (dorm) close to the school that he was attending in Tel-Aviv, Roberto was at the *maon studentim* (university dorm) at the University of Haifa, and I was at the Gan Shmuel Kibbutz close to the city of Hadera where I studied Hebrew and worked for four months. We would never again all live together, not in the same city, not in the same country. Neither would I have imagined that years later, while writing this story, my entire family would be dispersed around the world, nor that we would establish roots in five different countries. My parents are in Argentina (they returned in mid 1977 after living in Israel for ten months), Roberto is in Brazil, Jorge in Norway, Paula in Israel,

Exile From Argentina: A Jewish Family and the Military
Dictatorship (1976–1983), 2nd Edition, pages 45–63.
Copyright © 2024 by Information Age Publishing
www.infoagepub.com

and I am in the United States. My parents' life plans evaporated: that their children live close to them so they could see their grandchildren.

Gan Shmuel, with nearly five hundred members and a few hundred other people including potential members, foreign volunteers, soldiers and the *ulpan* (a program which allowed you to study Hebrew and which required four hours of work daily), was big enough to make the kibbutz feel like a small town. Gan Shmuel was one of the richest *kibbutzim* and its main source of income was a multi-million dollar factory that processed citric fruits and was a big exporter, at which many of the volunteers and those of us in the *úlpan* worked. It also owned a big supermarket, which was located on the highway close to the kibbutz. Gan Shmuel is renowned for all the artists and politicians that it introduced to the state of Israel. Like the great majority of the *kibbutzim*, Gan Shmuel maintained a strict socialist economy where the property, infrastructure and the means of production were community owned. I won't go into further detail about the kibbutz or the daily life of its members in this book because I have very little to add to what Jo-Ann Mort and Gary Brenner describe in their book *Our Hearts Invented a Place*.

Being in Israel towards the end of 1976 and the beginning of 1977 was not easy for me. It was very hard to both study Hebrew and work at the orange juice factory in the kibbutz at the same time. Soon after arriving at Gan Shmuel, I realized that the *Sochnut* (Jewish Agency) had sent me with a group of mainly young Argentineans. Most of them had left because of political problems. They were a group of "rajados" (escapees) which is what we called the people who had gone to Israel because of political problems as opposed to by free will. Some of these kids had been tortured or had family members who had disappeared.

One of these kids was Daniel Tarnopolsky. In later years, he would win a multimillion dollar suit for damages against Admiral Massera. His entire family had disappeared. Similar to my family, a lot of these kids' houses had undergone raids, had relatives that had disappeared or they had been kidnapped and tortured by the military.

In his book *Los chicos del exilio*, Tarnopolsky, who arrived at Gan Shmuel a few weeks before I did, tells about how when he got to the airport in Tel-Aviv, the emissaries of the Sochnut (Jewish Agency) "took [him] to the kibbutz [...] and they explained to [him] what they were going to do: that [he] was going to the "ulpam" [sic] to study Hebrew, that [he] was going to work and that after four months [he] was going to go to college. That was the plan. Everyone spoke English with broken accents. And, all of a sudden, two guys asked [him], "Where are you coming from?" He answered, "From Argentina," and there they switched from English to Spanish. "You're coming from Argentina?", "Yes, from Buenos Aires", "Oh, so are we. There are forty of us", and of those forty, they point out to [him], three were Zionists and the rest were not [...]. [He] didn't know anyone in the kibbutz "Gan Schmuel" [sic], but later others he knew showed up and that's when [Daniel's] world came together. But it was terrible in the "Gan Schmuel" [sic]. It was so sad."

In *Los chicos del exilio* Daniel also writes about how in Gan Shmuel, in 1976, Argentina's political climate at the time was well known. They knew what was going on within the first few months, about the kidnappings, about people being tortured and disappearing, "because a few of the people there had been activists and they began to better explain to [him] the deal with being an activist and with the kidnappings. It was already known. There was even one that had been kidnapped and then had reappeared. [Daniel] became very good friends with a guy, who now lives in France, who had been imprisoned along with his brother in La Plata; they weren't activists and yet they had been kidnapped. He had a sister and a brother-in-law, who were activists, but they hadn't been kidnapped; they had managed to escape. They had kidnapped him and his brother. They were in a sheriff's office in La Plata where they were tortured and then were released. They were lucky. He explained to [Daniel] what kidnapping and torture was."

Without a doubt, the Argentineans at Gan Shmuel were a problematic group since most of us had gone to Israel as a result of political problems. Furthermore, many had come to Israel without being Zionists, including some who claimed to be anti-Zionists. Others, as is my case, had stopped being Zionists shortly after arriving. When we were confronted with that everyday reality we discovered the faults of our expectations which were based on an idealism acquired through the Zionist youth movements in Argentina, be it leftwing or rightwing–Ichud Habonim, Dror, Hashomer Hatzair or Betar.

At first, my attitude towards Israel and Zionism was that of those kids who had belonged to Zionist youth movements in Argentina, who had left the protection of their middle or high-class homes. Somehow, we were hoping that life in Israel would be a continuation of the summer camps and the seminars in the winter which we attended when we were members of the Ichud or some other Zionist youth movement.

Even though Zionist values were lacking in a great part of the Argentineans at Gan Shmuel and in the *mechina* of the Hebrew University of Jerusalem, there were many supportive people working for the Jewish Agency at the student dorms of Giva Hatzorfatit (French Hill) and at *maon* Reznik towards the end of 1976 and through mid 1977. These people were mainly

Argentineans who tried to help us by providing social and psychological support so we could better adapt to our new circumstances. I particularly remember the help provided by other exiles that were older and had more experience, who would come visit us at the kibbutz and, starting in February of 1977, at the University in Jerusalem: the author and political scientist José Itzigsohn, the writer and journalist Ismael Viñas (brother to the famous author and professor at the University of Buenos Aires, David Viñas), Edy Kaufman, who was an Argentinean professor at the departments of Latin American Studies and Political Science at the Hebrew University of Jerusalem, who had lived in Israel since 1960, and the personnel who worked for the *mechina* in Jerusalem.

I dearly remember Moshe Fass, the director of the *mechina*. Fass patiently listened to all my complaints against the *mechina*, against Israel and against everything. He listened to me with a deep understanding and accepted that I wasn't exactly the ideal student. I also fondly remember Daniela, my academic counselor. She was French and spoke Spanish very well, but with a terrible accent. Even though I probably deserved to be kicked out of the university, Fass and Daniela didn't expel me from the *mechina*. On the contrary, they allowed me to stay at the student dorms of the University of Jerusalem, the *maon* Reznik, until I finished the program in July of 1977. I had stopped attending class since I had gotten back from a month-long trip through the Sinai desert and the Red Sea at the end of April. Even with all the support and help I got from the kind people who were willing to help me I was very confused and depressed. I could not manage to concentrate and study for class; it was also very hard for me to think about getting a job and working so I could support myself.

During those times, there was a sense of alienation amongst the Argentineans who had had to leave the country quickly and by force. In many cases, anything concerning Israel and political Zionism was received with negative, irrational and even a mocking attitude. I find it interesting that some of those who resented Zionism and were anti-Zionists had at some point been members and sometimes even leaders of Zionist-socialist movements in Argentina. In his *Memorias*, Enrique Gorriarán Merlo writes that, "In 1974 a group of fifty young Jewish kids joined PRT-ERP in Córdoba. They were members of organizations that defined themselves as Zionists and socialists. Some members had met in 1973 through groups in the universities that were linked to their project. Everyone went on to develop projects on different political fronts and, after being identified, were pursued with rancor by a particularly anti-Semitic regime." Mario Sznaider and Luis Roniger in the book *Represión y destierro: Itinerarios del exilio Argentino*, reveal that in later years, in 1976, "[J]ews whose families had been detained and disappeared resorted to, in their desperation and search for help, the representatives of the Jewish Agency and the consulate and the diplomats of Israel that were in Argentina. On the other hand, very quickly, people of Jewish origin that were being pursued or felt threatened by the wave of terror and persecution that was enveloping Argentina, also began to turn to the representatives already mentioned for help." It is also interesting that, according to Sznaider and Roniger in the same book, "even before the military coup in 1976, there were attempts to 'rescue' young Jews who had joined the left-wing movement—within and out of Peronism and who, in some cases, were giving in to the guerrillas. Nahum Solán, the representative of the Zionist Organization of the Zionist-Socialist youth party MAPAM at that time [...] traveled in 1975 to Argentina for three months, sent by the Jewish Agency and tried, once there, to contact the teens that had switched from the Zionist-socialist groups to the left-wing movements like the ERP and Montoneros [...]. He traveled to Córdoba where he found about twenty kids under these circumstances. He convinced twelve of them to opt to get out of it by moving to Israel."

At Gan Shmuel they had placed me in the advanced Hebrew class thanks to the large amount of Hebrew I learned at the Bialik School of La Plata. There I met a guy older than me who was about 25 years old, whom I met in the Ichud when I was thirteen or fourteen years old and they called him "la Chacha" because he was ugly and looked older than the rest of the people his age. Before joining the Montoneros, "la Chacha" had been the *mazkir* (secretary general) of the Ichud. In 1976, with the aide of the Embassy, he and his wife Cristina had fled to Israel. In Gan Shmuel there were several Argentineans who, like "la Chacha" and I, had not only been activists in Zionist movements, but had also had a Jewish education. That's why the language and many of the typically Israeli cultural experiences were not foreign to us. Neither were songs like *Lu Iehi, Yerushalaim shel Zahav* and we even knew modern Israeli rock songs from the Kaveret band and from famous Israeli singers Arik Einstein and Hava Alberstein.

Of the unpleasant memories that I have from the *mechina* at the Jewish University of Jerusalem there is one that stands out in particular. It was the night that I discovered that the Mossad (the intelligence service of Israel) had been closely watching some Argentinean kids who had been activists of the Montoneros, a leftist guerilla group which maintained contact with the Palestine Liberation Organization (PLO). That night, in March of 1977, Pablo, my roommate from the student dorms on Mevo Dakar 4 Street at the Givá Hatzorfatit (French Hill), woke me up in a very agitated state, scared, and almost crying. Pablo immediately told me that he had been an activist for the Montoneros and that he had just spent the entire night being questioned by the Mossad. He told me that they didn't hit him or torture him, but that the men who had questioned him insisted that he knew things about the Montonero activists of Jewish origin who were at the time training in Lebanon with the Palestinians of the PLO. They also asked him to spy on his Argentinean classmates of the *mechina* at the University of Jerusalem to see if there was someone keeping in touch with the Palestinians. That had not been the first time Pablo had had contact with the security services of Israel. That same night he told me that a few months earlier, while visiting the Mishmar Haemek kibbutz where he was a volunteer, some soldiers had hit him because he had innocently decided to take some photographs of a military base close to Beer Sheva in the desert of Negev. A few weeks later the Mosad had interrogated him, Pablo left Israel and went to Spain and then returned to Argentina. Later on a friend of mine saw him on vacation in Pinamar with his girlfriend.

At that time I thought that Pablo had gone crazy and that he had been imagining things. I couldn't get it into my head that there could be Jewish kids training in Lebanon or cooperating with the PLO. I also couldn't believe that the Israeli intelligence was keeping tabs on the Argentinean students of the *mechina*. It was a big surprise for me, while I was writing this book, when I discovered in the book *El tren de la victoria* by Cristina Zucker (Marcos Zucker's daughter, the famous Jewish-Argentinean actor) that the actor's son had been in Lebanon receiving military training and that, in general, it was true that there had been young Jews training with the PLO in the 1970s. Fito, one of Cristina Zucker's sources, talks about how, "in Lebanon [...] [e]veryone [would] laugh when Pato [Zucker] would cover up so people couldn't tell that he was circumcised, but for the Palestinians it was prideful that there were Jews sharing their cause [...]. There were plenty of files from the Argentinean intelligence on this subject [...]. The Palestinians preferred not to be noticed too much: a group of Argentineans running around in the country [was] like a fly in the milk [...] In regards to the work of the intelligence that might have been gathered by the Mossad, or 'the academy', as they typically call the Israeli intelligence, to identify them, Fito admits that they sometimes thought about it, but [they trusted] that when [they were going to leave] there, [they were going to] change their passports to get into the country."

Years later, in October of 1980, when I was studying English and French at the Hebrew University of Jerusalem, I received a letter form the Irgun Leshituf Habeinleumí (the Organization for International Cooperation) inviting me to a job interview in Tel-Aviv. The letter said that someone had recommended me for the job. They asked me to go to an address in Tel-Aviv and to take my Argentine passport with me. I remember that I showed the letter to Osnat—a classmate of mine, who at that time was in the reserves of the army's information services and who now-a-days works for Interpol—and she told me that she was sure that "the Mossad or one of the Israeli security services sent the letter." With immature expectations I thought that, like in action movies, they were going to offer me an interesting, well-paying job. I went to the "job interview." In the room there were three guys sitting behind a desk, a chair placed about a meter away from the desk so I could sit down, and two guys standing behind me close to the door. They asked me if I had military experience and I answered that I did. I had just finished my military service in the naval forces of Argentina. One of the interviewers said to me, "You're an intelligent guy and you know several languages. We want to offer you a job working for the country [Israel]." I asked him, "What kind of job?", and he said to me, "First we need you to give us your Argentine passport for a few days." I said to him, "I don't want to." At that moment, one of the men said, "This interview is over." A few minutes later I was on the street, heading to the bus terminal in Tel-Aviv so I could return to Jerusalem.

In early April of 1977 I hitchhiked through Sinai to spend the week of *Pesach* (Passover) in Nueiba, a beach on the Red Sea, with a group of Argentines. These were friends from La Plata from the Ichud times who were volunteering in the Or Haner kibbutz or studying in the *machon le madrichim* (the institute of the Jewish Agency in Jerusalem for the development of leaders of youth Zionist movements across the world). At that time the beach still belonged to Israel and today is part of, along with Dahab and Sharm El Sheich, the "Red Sea Riviera" that belongs to Egypt.

During my stay at the Nueiba beach, I ate pita bread, oranges and other things that I bought from the Bedouins that appeared like a mirage every morning in the Sinai desert. I brought water in a bottle that I filled up from a tap that was about two kilometers away from where I had set up my sleeping bag. I had everything I needed. That was a week of new and gratifying experiences: sleeping on the beach, swimming in the sea, forgetting about time and the world in general. The most important thing of that time period was that for the first time, in a long time, I was able to think about coming up with a plan of action and adapting to the new circumstances of my life. I was getting used to the idea that it was very possible that I would never live with my parents again, or even in Argentina. I started to realize that I had to create new frames of reference in order to adapt to this new reality. I still hadn't thought of the possibility that I could live in a country that wasn't Argentina or Israel.

When the week of vacation was over, when it was time to go back to class in Jerusalem, I couldn't muster the necessary strength (which at that time seemed like it needed to be superhuman) to get on the bus that would take me back. I made one of the most important decisions in my life, and for the first time ever, I did it on my own. I stayed in the Nueiba beach for almost a month until I got tired of being alone and not doing anything. When I got tired of the sea and the sand I returned to Jerusalem, but I decided not to return to the university, or at least not to attend class. But even though I stopped going to class, I still lived in the Reznik student dorm, in Mount Scopus. I let my beard and hair grow long like Roger Daltrey in "Tommy," and I dedicated my time to thinking about my life, spending hours talking with other Argentines and people of other countries. We talked about life and the world that we were living in, trying to find ideas that would help me decide what I wanted to do and where I wanted to go.

At that time, also for the first time in my life, I realized the necessity of earning a living for myself. I was surrounded by peers who focused on studying and working in order to be able to buy food, pay rent and cover their basic needs. Some of them had wealthy parents who would provide for themselves and didn't have to work. Since my parents couldn't give me any money, I had to work and live modestly, even though at the time I didn't let my financial situation affect my way of thinking or of appreciating life. It wasn't easy. Aside from a small scholarship from the Israeli government, no one else could help me. The scholarship and a small sum of money that I earned working at the *Sifria Leumit* (the National Library) (on the Givat Ram campus of the Jewish University) was barely enough to pay for my student housing at Reznik. I remember that I was jealous of some of the Argentine kids whose parents sent them money for living and travel expenses during the vacations, not only to Argentina (for those who wanted to go home to visit), but also to Europe, the U.S., South Africa, and other places.

Back then, like in Moris' song, I didn't have much to eat. Practically all I ate was pasta with butter, sausages and *hummus* with bread that I bought at the supermarket, and raisins and dates that were cheap at the *shuk* (Arab market) in the old city of Jerusalem. Sometimes I would treat myself with a plate of *hummus* or falafel at a food stand downtown or at the *shuk*. At other times some of my Argentine friends who were volunteers at a kibbutz would come and visit me, bringing with them fruits, coffee and some Dubeks, which were very cheap cigarettes that they would get for free at the *kibbutzim*. Sometimes when I would go and visit my parents in Haifa, I would bring back with me eggs, tomatoes, butter and bread that my mother got from the *merkaz klita* kitchen.

As I previously mentioned, during those months I found a job classifying and placing books back on the shelves in the basement of the *Sifria Leumit*. My roommate Pablo from the *mechina* who had worked at the library for a while got me the job. Without a doubt, that was the most boring job I have ever had. At that time there were quite a few Argentines that were working in the basement of the *Sifria Leumit*. When we could no longer bear the boredom of shelving books, we would pass the time smoking and discussing Argentine and Israeli politics or we would simply sit on the floor, and, instead of putting the books away we would read them when we found one that interested us.

In August of 1977, a few days before my parents went back to Argentina with my brother Jorge and my sister Paula, and before Roberto and I were left alone in Israel, I experienced a very traumatic event that changed my life radically: Roberto, Jorge, an Argentine friend from Gan Shmuel and I almost drowned. That day we decided to swim in the caves of Rosh Hanikra, at the Lebanese border. These caves open up to the sea and only when we were in the water did we realize that we would have to swim many kilometers to get to the shore. I remember that once we were underwater I began to panic and it was only a miracle that the four of us were able to climb up onto a rock. We stayed there until professional divers of the Special Forces of the Israeli Marines came and rescued us. They were friends of Roberto and lived in the Rosh Hanikra kibbutz where my brother had lived for almost a year. Even today I close my eyes and see myself drowning in a violent sea, my hands and feet covered in blood because of the cuts caused by the rocks, which I tried to hold on to so I would not sink. I remember that Jorge was holding on to me by my hair, which at that time was very long, and that him along with Roberto and our friend were helping me get up on to the ledge of the rock. Meanwhile, my parents had called the kibbutz and that was when they sent the Israeli Marines, who were expert swimmers in any type of situation. I came out badly hurt, with my hands and feet all cut up from the sharp and jagged rocks that I was trying to hang on to so I wouldn't drown. For me that was the end of my adolescence. This was when I first realized that I was not immortal.

When I was almost nineteen, in addition to the trauma of leaving Argentina and the hardships of living in a foreign country, I had also discovered that I was mortal. I had barely made it out alive. But the most important thing that I realized at the time was that all I had done up until then was go to school and to the Ichud. I felt that I hadn't lived a lot and that I didn't have a story, that my life was an empty book. For many months following the experience, I had recurring nightmares that I was drowning in the caves of Rosh Hanikra.

A few days after this had happened, my parents returned to Argentina and Roberto and I went to work as volunteers at the Kfar Blum kibbutz in the Galilee, close to the city of Kiriat Shmona. I had a very good experience in Kfar Blum. I was living with a nice group of guys and girls that were all from different countries. I met people from all over the world at that kibbutz: there were British, Irish, Swiss, Dutch, Scandinavian and South African volunteers as well as some from other countries, but there were no Argentines or people from South America.

In Kfar Blum I learned some English and I also began losing interest in Argentine, Israeli and global politics. There I began to be interested in existential subjects and in traveling and seeing and learning about other cultures. I felt that at that moment I was starting a new stage in life, a stage of traveling and adventures. A few years earlier, while in La Plata, I had read a book that, since my stay at Kfar Blum, was an important guide to my new way of living and thinking since my life changing experience. The book was *The Road to Katmandu* by René Barjavel. In it, Oliver, the main character, is a student leader in France in May of 1968 who for a month participates in the student strike of the Sorbonne and in political discussions with workers and students. When he realizes that that idea of a revolution is only an illusion, he decides to change a sign that said "permanent discussion" (which he had written himself) to one that said "finished discussion", and he goes on a journey to Katmandu in search of a different existential and geographic destiny. Just like Oliver, I also hung up a sign that said "finished discussion" and I began a journey that continues even until today.

At that time, for the first time in a while, I began to have fun and enjoy myself. We volunteers organized activities all the time. We had dance parties, played soccer, and went to the swimming pool of the kibbutz at night. Even though the work, like in Gan Shmuel, was tiring and tedious, I enjoyed working at Kfar Blum. I spent most of the time in that kibbutz working outside picking apples which began at five in the morning and finished at one in the afternoon. We had a half-hour break at ten in the morning so we could eat and swim in the Jordan River, which goes through the apple farm, with other volunteers. The houses in which we lived were old wooden cabins with a community bathroom outside. The food was abundant and of good quality, although the choices were somewhat monotonous. The volunteers would eat at the *chadar ochel* (a cafeteria) along with some of the members of the kibbutz. Most of the time we had vegetables, salad, eggs, pasta, dairy products and of course apples and other fruit that the kibbutz grew. The only meat they served was chicken either in a soup or as meatballs. On Fridays the food was always better since they served roasted chicken and some dessert or cake.

The kibbutz gave us a monthly allowance of about $50 dollars, which we mainly spent on Time cigarettes, which were better than the free Dubek cigarettes that we got. They would also give us stamps and stationery, Turkish and instant coffee and tea; they gave us work clothes and they would do our laundry. I won't go into the details of the routines and daily life of a volunteer in the Israeli kibbutz in this book since I don't have much to add to the magnificent painting of the daily life of a foreign volunteer that Todd Natenberg paints in his memories: *The Journey within: Two Months in Kibbutz,* and to the detailed sociological study of a doctoral student from Hebrew University of Jerusalem about foreign volunteers in the *kibbutzim* written by David Mittleberg: *Strangers in Paradise: The Israeli Kibbutz Experience.*

In Kfar Blum, I began to listen to music that was different from what I had heard before: rock in English—Procol Harum, Moody Blues, and Alice Cooper, among others—and I stopped listening to Argentine rock. This change had begun a few months before when I was in the *mechina* of Jerusalem. At the *mechina* I became close friends with two girls, one American and one Australian, both of them, funnily enough, named Linda. With these two girls I listened to music that they had brought with them to Israel, mainly Bob Dylan, Neil Young, Crosby, Stills, Nash & Young, Judy Collins, Joni Mitchell and other singers from the '60s and '70s. The American girl had lived in Miami her entire life and spoke Spanish very well. She had had many classmates in school that were Cuban who had left Cuba because of the communist revolution of Fidel Castro. A few months later a Nicaraguan guy, whose parents had sent him to study in Israel to escape the revolution in Nicaragua, introduced me to the music of The Doors.

One day when we were listening to music, I asked the American girl if she would like to listen to Argentine rock: Los Gatos, Almendra, and Sui Generis. She said she would and I put in the cassette player what was for me the *summum* of Argentine rock: *Confesiones de invierno* by Sui Generis. After listening carefully to the entire cassette she told me, not very delicately, that this music seemed childish to her and she was surprised that someone my age would like these songs. I didn't dare to play the big hits by Los Gatos or by Almendra, which I also had. An album that she did like was the *Cantata Santamaría de Iquique* by the Quilapayún, a famous Chilean protest group. The Australian girl, who did not speak Spanish, agreed with the American girl when I translated my favorite Sui Generis songs into Hebrew. At the time the American girl listened not only to Bob Dylan and Neil Young, but she also liked Bruce Springsteen who in Argentina in 1977 had never been heard. Even though I never stopped liking Argentine rock, I would never again refer to it as "national rock." Around that time I began listening more to rock in English. Today I have a collection of approximately 1,500 albums, which includes more than 1,000 CDs of rock in English and about 300 of Argentine rock.

In Kfar Blum I met Bernadette, a beautiful blue-eyed redhead from Northern Ireland, who was two years older than me, had lived all her life in the Catholic neighborhood of Belfast, and who soon became my girlfriend. At the time Bernadette and I had a lot in common. Just like me, she had also had trouble with the military that dominated her country and she belonged to a minority religion. We were both coming from living a violent period in our own lives and in the history of our countries. She had been affected by the conflict in Northern Ireland, the trouble in the Ulster, and I by the dictatorship in Argentina in the '70s.

Spending our days with people from Europe and the United States, Bernadette and I realized that living in environments with political violence, like the ones we had come from was not something normal. We appreciated the freedom that the kibbutz represented for us, amongst volunteers, where no one was attacked or criticized for their political or religious views.

Bernadette and I were friends with John, an American who was my age and had lived all his life in New York. The three of us arrived to Kfar Blum at about the same time. Recently, I got in touch with him through e-mail. He is now an architect and still lives in New York. I asked him if he remembers Bernadette and me and if Kfar Blum had changed his life in any way. Sometime later, John sent me an e-mail back (New York, 4/17/03):

> It was a pleasure to read your warm and generous e-mail. I needed some time to digest, reflect, and answer; this afternoon at Seder [a religious ceremony marking Passover] was the perfect moment [...]. It is wonderful that you are taking the time to write your memories. Of course that year changed my life, the motives and intentions of our lives. It is like a dream which appears from time to time, and all at once, in an unexpected way. I ended up spending almost a year in the kibbutz completely by chance. I graduated 49th out of a class of 50 and had no desire to go to college. My father, even though he was Jewish, wasn't particularly Zionist and wasn't interested in his Jewish identity. But he was the one who recommended that I go live in a kibbutz as a means of traveling and working abroad. I didn't do my bar mitzvah, nor did I have a religious need to go to Israel. But the history, the scenery, the myths and who knows what else had their effect on me, in ways that would only become clear later on. As a kid, living in New York City, in the '60s and '70s, the political assassinations, Vietnam and riots formed the background I grew up with. But somehow that all seemed so distant and abstract. Israel made history come to life, "as if it had happened to me"—as it says in the Haggada [religious book that tells the story of the Jews leaving Egypt]. The months that I spent in [Kfar Blum] were the beginning of an education where I taught myself, Jewish history, Holocaust, Zionism, the Arab-Israeli conflict, etc. Reading of course was

important, but more important was the people. I liked what you wrote to me about Bernadette. I remember her vividly, the passion and pain that she carried with her because of the conflict in Northern Ireland. It was a surprise to me; I had never met a person who had been so hurt and that could be that way, full of hate [...]. It was stimulating to learn, see, and share that experience with someone else [...]. I remember years ago while reading Timerman's book and thinking, "I wonder what happened with Dani."

I left Kfar Blum in October. Shortly after Bernadette went to visit me in Jerusalem, at the student residence in Reznik where my brother Roberto, who at the time had started studying history, had his own room. Roberto was very generous to leave it for the two of us. Bernadette and I were together for four days, walking around Jerusalem and visiting historical Christian, Jewish, and Muslim sites. We also went to the Holocaust museum at Yad Vashem and we went to see the Chagall vitraux at the Hadassah hospital. Bernadette then returned to Kfar Blum and a few days later I followed her. I worked as a volunteer once again for a couple of weeks, but I had to leave again shortly. Yaffa, the person in charge of the volunteers, had me kicked out of Kfar Blum for trying to organize a strike. I insisted that it was unfair that only the volunteers had to do the dirty jobs that the members of the kibbutz refused to do like spending an entire day shoveling rotten, smelly chickens that died during the night due to power outages and the poor ventilation system.

At the end of October I went back to Jerusalem where I spent a few nights on the floor of Roberto's room in the student dorm. I remember that Roberto had a Colombian roommate who sometimes brought his Argentine girlfriend to spend the night. At the time Roberto also had an Argentine girlfriend. It was chaos. I realized that it was impossible for me to stay there any longer.

Without a place to stay and with very little money, I hitchhiked my way to Or Haner, a kibbutz that was founded by Argentines of Ichud Habonim, in the Negev desert, to which some of my *madrichim* (leaders of the Ichud) had emigrated. I was accepted in Or Haner thanks to the recommendation of a guy from Santa Fe who they called Gilligan, because of his resemblance to the T.V. character. He was married to Dafne, a girl from La Plata. They let me stay as a temporary volunteer for about three weeks until a group of Scandinavians arrived. They actually didn't have room for me, but thanks to Gilligan I had a place to stay for a few weeks. A few days before the Scandinavians arrived I went back to Jerusalem, where I stayed until the end of December 1977, staying in my friends' rooms in Reznik and sometimes in my friend David Mibashan's apartment which he shared with an Israeli. At the time David worked as a cashier at the Hilton hotel. Our arrangement was that for three or four nights out of the week, when he had to work a night shift, I was allowed to use his bed until seven in the morning; after seven when David came back, I would move over to the couch in the living room.

In January of 1978 I stayed in the Ein Harod Meuchad kibbutz in the Galilee, where I worked until the beginning of March as a *madrich* (guide) to a group of Brazilians who went to spend the summer in Israel working in an orange field. They participated in the *Tapuz* (orange) volunteer program that was managed by the Jewish Agency, for young Latin Americans from the south, mainly Argentines and Brazilians, but also Chileans. They would pick oranges or do other work in a kibbutz in Israel for two months during the South American summer.

In the two months that I worked at the Ein Harod kibbutz I was able to save about $1000 dollars, which was quite a fortune for me at the time.

In the beginning of March of 1978 I returned to Jerusalem where I worked as a messenger for a travel agency called Dafna Tours. I really enjoyed this job because the agency gave me a *kartisia* (a weekly pass) to ride the buses for free and I would spend all morning wandering the city picking up airplane tickets and taking them to the customer's house. I worked from eight in the morning until noon. Actually, they paid me to do what I most liked at the time, which was to wander the city. After work, I would take a nap everyday and almost everyday I would go to the movie theatre in *maon* Reznik where they showed a different movie every night for very cheap. Sometimes I would go to the Reznik *moadon* (club) to visit my brother Roberto and to meet some friends.

At the time I had become pretty good friends with a very intelligent girl, Paula Resnitzky, who was also a regular at the Reznik *moadon*. Paula and her brother Marcos were the children of Nehemías Resnitzky, who was president of the Delegation of Israelite Associations of Argentina. Marcos told me that he had personally suffered from the dictatorship. At the end of July in 1977 a group of militia men had tortured him for a week. The torturers accused him of taking part in an international conspiracy of the Jews to dominate Argentina and the world through a combination of American capitalism, Russian bolshevism, and Israeli Zionism. As "proof" that Marcos was part of the conspiracy they wanted him to explain why he had recently visited New York City, Jerusalem, and Moscow along with his father, as if his traveling to those cities, where there were large Jewish communities, was solid proof that Marcos was part of an international conspiracy by the Jews.

Even though I had not been much of a drinker up until that point, I started going to a bar called Tavern regularly in downtown Jerusalem. I would also frequent the Danish coffee-shop, in the *shuk* of the old city, to go have some Turkish coffee with the Arabs and the European and American hippies who were regulars there. I lived in an apartment on Haim Haviv 6 Street in Kiriat Hayovel, a working class neighborhood; I had gotten a small room that was actually a closet that my friend David Mibashan sublet to me for $30 dollars a month. The apartment was dirty and it had no heating or hot water and I slept on a mattress on the floor inside a sleeping bag.

Towards the end of March of 1978 my parents sent me money to buy a ticket to return to Argentina. With that money and what I earned while working as a *madrich* in the *Tapuz* program in the kibbutz Ein Harod and as a messenger for the Dafna Tours traveling agency, I went to Denmark in late April of 1978. It was the year of the famous World Cup that took place in Argentina, during the middle of the dictatorship.

Rubén Saferstein was one my Argentine friends who I saw frequently at the time. We were classmates in the *mechina* and we lived in the same student residence halls at the University of Jerusalem in 1977, first in Giva Hatzor-fatit and then in Reznik. Later, Rubén became close friends with my brother Roberto and we continued seeing each other for many years. Today Rubén is a rabbi in a middle class Jewish community, Dor Chadash, located in the neighborhood of Once in Buenos Aires.

In a conversation (Buenos Aires, 9/25/03) with Rubén Saferstein, he tells me of the events that took place in his life while he lived in Israel and also of his current life in Buenos Aires:

EDF: How did you decide to go to Israel?

R: I left in January of 1977. My family was part of the middle class. We were comfortable; my dad was an accountant. My mom dedicated herself to administrative duties. I went to a private school. I was raised as a child in the Bet El community, very close to Rabbi Marshall Meyer. My mom, along with my uncle and grandfather, worked in offices. In 1976, the dictatorship, because of economic extortion, was looking for a person we knew because he worked with my uncle, my mom and my grandfather. I was 18. We were very scared and we went to an uncle's house in Buenos Aires. Every day we would go around our house to see what was going on. At the same time, my mother's psychoanalyst's son disappeared. It was the first case of someone disappearing that we heard of. I wasn't politically involved. It was in March on 1976. I never dealt with it personally nor did my mother. Because of the economic extortion, my parents suggested that I go study abroad, that I was 18, and to be 18 in 1976 was dangerous. It was seen as a dangerous thing. It was during that time that a small delegation of the Hebrew University headed by a physics professor named Labaton came to Argentina. He was at a presentation in Bet El [a synagogue of Jewish reformist movement] and he motivated a few people, Dani, Darío, Judit and I to travel to Israel together and that way we would travel to study in the *mechiná* [a prep school for college] in Spanish. We went as a group, without doing the kibbutz ulpan [program to study Hebrew]. None of us had been activists. We simply had gone to Bet El. It was getting to *mechina* and meeting people we didn't know from Buenos Aires and from other places like Bahía Blanca, Córdoba, and La Plata, people with different backgrounds, and beginning to meet people who had their stories, like Dani Tarnopolsky. People like Beto, Dani, you, that for us, people who had gone to Bet El, who had never had had anything to do with politics or activism, it was a good starting point for getting to know a different reality to which one had been a stranger. Our deal with the Sochnut [Jewish Agency] was through regular means, just going to study in Israel. It is very different to do the paperwork with the minhal hastudentim [the office for students of the Jewish Agency] than from having to speed up the paperwork. I remember when I went to the police station to pick up my passport, there had been a violent incident; I decided that I was not going back to Argentina. I used to wish that I had never lived in Argentina. Reality for me was that I had lived in Israel for five years, I got my BA and on two occasions I went back to Argentina for a vacation, in 1979 for the youth tournament in Japan and in 1978 after the World Cup. I watched the World Cup while in Israel and then I visited Argentina for the summer vacation. There were some things that I hadn't finished taking care of. I decided to return to Argentina temporarily. I hadn't really planned to leave Israel.

EDF: Did you suffer any losses having left Argentina in 1977?

R: In the distance, over time, there were some losses. I had a brother who was in his sophomore year of high school with whom I lost touch for the first five years that I was abroad; I cut off the relationship with him. We didn't live together, nor did I live with my parents. In that sense, the loss had to do with family life. It was a loss for me to leave my grandparents. I didn't see it as a loss to leave the cafés or the culture, or missing the Spanish language or soccer. That I didn't feel at all. I don't feel that I really lost anything. On the contrary; I started to take care of myself, wash my own clothes, and cook my own food. I really enjoyed the Hebrew

University because I was always a book lover and I was able to see a room full of books. I felt very happy being in the *mechina* with about ninety other people, all dedicated to similar things. I also had family that I could visit in Israel. I felt that during that time I grew a lot.

EDF: How do you feel about that experience nowadays?

R: It was a very trying experience, leaving a life of comfort, even though I was not deprived while I lived in Israel. It was my father's and Bet El's initiative that got me there even though I had a calm life and thought that nothing was going to happen to me. I was unaware of the things that were going on around me. In Israel one was illuminated. Seeing and speaking of the concentration camps, having heard of cases such as that of Tarnopolsky and Resnitzky in Israel. On a trip to London I went to a bookstore where they sold pamphlets and posters that had to do with the dictatorships in various countries, and I remember seeing there a poster of the World Cup of '78 in Argentina which was of a cup and flag and instead of a soccer ball there was Videla's face. I bought those posters and here I was having met Marshall Meyer and in Israel having met Timerman and his son with whom I became close friends. I also heard the Uruguayan Daniel Vigilietti's songs in Israel. The Uruguayans there also introduced me to Zitarrosa's music, music that I was not used to. Songs by Violeta Parra or Víctor Jara, things of that sort. I started leaning more towards the left wing. And as a rabbi I feel obliged to these people. My wife came from a family that was involved in politics. Her boyfriend's house had been raided. There was also my commitment with the left wing, because of my social work.

EDF: Did your relationship to Argentina change because of your experience in Israel?

R: One thing that changed was that I started seeing a woman who was not Jewish. It would have been some sort of rebellious act to try certain things. Coming back to Argentina it was as if one was more open to these things. Even though I don't feel like a nationalist of the Republic of Argentina. I feel like an inhabitant of a world where I get to experience today. I don't know for how long. Today it is here and with this congregation. I see how people from all over the world are alike. The Jewish communities are very similar all over the world, like the one in Canada for example. Not having gone to a Jewish school, rather to a British school, and getting close to Bet El during my teenage years allowed me to view Judaism in a different way. I was not a product of a Zionist movement. I didn't go to Israel because of political problems.

EDF: What do you remember of our time spent in college?

R: From my memories of you I remember you as a crazy guy. What we call here "un tiro al aire" (a loose cannon). I remember meeting a couple of brothers because there weren't many brothers like you and Roberto in the *mechina*. I was able to compare one to the other. Roberto was applied, dedicated and studious and you, besides your form of expressing yourself, there was no way of stopping you, you were very talkative, your way of dressing, always wearing mismatched clothes. I remember that shirt of yours that was too big for you everywhere, it was very informal, to see that the Israeli summer style of shorts and sandals suited you. As if they were playing your game. It was harder for others, those that lived on your floor. It was you that lived with that guy who got shot in the heel. What I admired about you was that you liked to read a lot. You were someone that read anything, all different kinds of literature, including Russian literature; I always have the image of you reading a book. It didn't make sense—because you were the opposite of an intellectual, you were against the university establishment—but I would never see you without a book in your hand or on your nightstand. It stuck with me that you never had any trouble saying anything you felt to whomever it may be; you weren't ashamed of saying whatever came to mind. I wasn't surprised when you started seeing the Irish girl. When you said that you were going to Denmark I said, "That's him." It still puzzles me, having heard about your activities in universities in the United States, when I picture you in a classroom because when I think of you I think of anti-establishment, of an anarchist, of an outsider. I find it hard to understand that you are a professor, that you have written and published books, it is hard for me to believe that it is the same person. When you started your first research and I think that it was the first time I heard you say "Papiamento," I got a fixed idea about what that language meant. Hearing you speak loosely about creole helped me understand your personal history with your son. These are very strong images that I have of you as a person. You had an affinity to books and literature. I would always see you going to the movie theatre, not the nightclubs. I saw you as a bohemian, as a hippie in Israel. That was you. I could never picture you with a coat and tie. I never thought that you would end up as a professor in a university in the United States, especially not in the United States. You could have ended up in Brazil, having married a Brazilian woman. I never imagined you in the United States, although you can also be anti-imperialist in the United States. You were someone, and this was the fun part for me, that was unpredictable.

In Denmark

Somewhere, somehow, somebody
Must have kicked you around some
Tell me why you wanna lay there
And revel in your abandon
Listen it don't make no difference to me baby
Everybody's had to fight to be free
Now baby you don't have to live like a refugee

—Tom Petty, *Refugee*

In late April of 1978 I went to Denmark. My Israeli temporary resident's visa had expired because I had dropped out of school, and because of this the Ministry of the Interior was looking for me to force me get my Israeli citizenship and to recruit me to the *tzava* (the Israeli army). The Irish girl that I dated in Kfar Blum, Bernadette, had invited me to go to Denmark. Bernadette had recently gone to Esbjerg, a city in the coast of the North Sea, where she lived with her sister Maura, her brother-in-law Joe and her nephew Brandon. Shortly after she arrived, Joe and Maura's second son Connor was born. Bernadette had a daughter, Nicola, who was my sister Paula's age and who was being taken care of by her grandparents in Belfast. In Esbjerg, towards the end of the '70s, there were many Irish immigrants who had gone to Belfast because of political problems or because they could not find work. She and her family were Catholics, and at that time the Irish Catholics were being oppressed by the British troops in Northern Ireland.

Exile From Argentina: A Jewish Family and the Military
Dictatorship (1976–1983), 2nd Edition, pages 65–69.

A few days before I arrived, Bernadette had rented a room on the second story of a house located at 17 Knudedybet Street, close to the downtown area, and close to a park that had a collection of modernist statues and a lake with ducks in it. We lived together in that house until 1979. We spent our time reading, listening to music, and writing in our journals. We had a small motorcycle and during the winter we would go downtown to the public library and check out books in English and Spanish, and English rock records. At that time I discovered the music of Leonard Cohen, David Bowie and ABBA, a Swedish group at the top of its career for the Scandinavians and for the rest of the world. I was very impressed that during this time a country could have a public library where you could check out music that had recently come out. That summer we spent a lot of time riding the motorcycle along the beaches on the coast of the North Sea, close to Esbjerg, where we would go sunbathing. I remember that I was very surprised when I saw a cement casement that the Nazis had built to protect the Danish coast during the Second World War that had remained intact since that time.

In September of 1978 we hitchhiked our way to Amsterdam. It took us one full day and night to get through the south of Denmark and the north of Germany, traveling on a highway that goes through Flensburg, Hamburg, Bremen and Rotterdam, until we got to Amsterdam. In Amsterdam we walked a lot, fascinated by everything we saw. We visited Anne Frank's house and I remember that I ate Chinese food for the first time in my life.

On my way back from Amsterdam the Danish guards stopped me at the German border. It was still the time of the European Community; the European Union did not exist yet, so one had to show their passport at every border including that between Germany and Denmark. I was taken aback when they didn't let me return to Denmark and they sent me to the Danish consulate in Flensburg to ask for a visa.

I lived there for nearly a month waiting for the visa. First I slept in a park and then I went to a youth hostel where I did household chores in exchange for a place to sleep and breakfast. Since I had no money, I would eat sandwiches for lunch and dinner made with the bread that I saved from breakfast and with sardine cans and mayonnaise packets that I lifted at a supermarket in Flensburg. The situation I was in was very unpleasant. The man in charge of the hostel was a refugee in Sweden during the Nazi period and he treated me like a son, but the other workers always looked at me badly. At that time, in Germany there were still a lot of people who had lived through the Nazi period. One day at the hostel I had a conflict with a Chilean-German Nazi who frequented Flensburg. This is the dialogue that occurred:

Ch: Are you Argentine?

EDF: Yes.

Ch: What are you doing here in Germany?

EDF: I'm waiting to get my visa to go to Denmark.

Ch: And if they don't give it to you?

EDF: I'll probably go back to Israel.

Ch: Are you Jewish?

EDF: Yes.

Ch: In another time they would have made soap out of you.

EDF: Why don't you go fuck yourself.

I waited patiently for the visa while I stayed at the hostel in Flensburg. I was sure that they would give it to me, since I had never been denied entrance to any other place. I couldn't imagine getting rejected for a visa to go to Denmark, a country in which I felt like I was at home and that I knew very well. After almost a month of waiting, I was taken set back again when I went to the Danish consulate and the consul, with a mocking tone, told me, "The Ministry of External Affairs of Denmark in Copenhagen has denied your visa to return to Esbjerg." I recall the following conversation that took place between the Danish consul and me at the Danish consulate in Flensburg in September of 1978:

C: Why would you like to visit Denmark?

EDF: I live in Denmark.

C: What do you do in Denmark?

EDF: I live in Denmark.

C: Copenhagen has denied your request for a visa.

EDF: Why? I want to live in Denmark. My girlfriend lives there.

C: And who are you?

I was furious as I left; the word *sudaca* ("spic") wasn't being used yet, but I already knew its meaning. It was clear that the Danish consul felt that way about me. But the fact that my visa was denied didn't stop me. That same day I crossed the border between Germany and Denmark illegally, hidden in the backseat of a Volkswagen Beetle, which belonged to a woman I had met at the hostel in Flensburg. I thus became an illegal immigrant in Europe.

Just as when I lifted sardine cans and packets of mayonnaise from the super-market, I did not feel any guilt when I crossed the border illegally; I had to survive somehow. I stayed in Denmark for a few more months, but I was no longer happy the way I was when I was there legally.

In January of 1979 I made a six hour roundtrip from Esbjerg to Co-penhagen to renew my Argentine passport, carrying with me only a salami sandwich, my expired passport, a passport photo without a beard, and 100 Danish Kroner to pay for the visa. After handing my passport to a girl and waiting for nearly two hours in the waiting room in the consulate, a man called me and told me, "kid, it's time for you to shave off your beard and go back to your country to serve your duty. Take your passport. You have ten days to return to the fatherland." Then he wrote on the passport itself, "Passport renewed for ten days only for the return to the Republic of Argen-tina." They had only renewed it for ten days! I had no way out, in a few days I would be back in Argentina to fulfill my military duty or I would be classified as a deserter and who knows when I would see my family again and be able to visit the country where I was born and raised.

In February of 1979, Nils Pedersen, a Danish reporter married to a wom-an from southern Ireland, who was a close friend of mine, offered to help me get political asylum and to help me live in Denmark legally so I could work or study and get my life back together. I thought about it carefully and politely refused. My instincts told me that staying in Denmark was worse than being part of the military in Argentina, even during the dictatorship. I decided to return to serve in the military. I said goodbye to Bernadette and to Denmark.

In late February of 1979, after having been out of Argentina for more than two years, I returned to the country in the middle of the dictatorship. I traveled for a week on train from Esbjerg to Lisbon, I stopped for two days in Paris, where I visited an American friend who I had met in Israel, and I took a flight from Lisbon to Rio de Janeiro. I got there without enough money to take a bus to Buenos Aires, but after asking for money and food for two days in the *rodoviaria* Novo Río, I got enough money to buy a ticket from the com-pany Pluma. In Israel they had advised me not to go into Argentina through the Ezeiza airport in Buenos Aires because of security issues. So, I decided to cross the border of Brazil and Argentina at the Foz de Iguazú by bus, mixing in with the Argentine tourists that were returning from their sum-mer vacations. After two days of traveling I arrived at the Constitución bus station in Buenos Aires. A very pretty Brazilian girl who was traveling with me from Rio and was also going to La Plata bought me a bus ticket to go to La Plata. I didn't have a cent on me. It was sweltering hot that afternoon in

February of 1979. When I close my eyes I remember it as if it were today. I walked to my parents' apartment on the corner of 8th and 48th, in central La Plata. In the few blocks between the station and the apartment, and as I passed by 47th Street, I smelled the oranges and saw the Liceo building, almost after three years of being away. It was one of the happiest feelings of my life. As I walked, I vividly remember crying the last few blocks.

In the BIM 3

Yo formé parte de un ejército loco
Tenía veinte años y el pelo muy corto
Pero, mi amigo, hubo una confusión
Porque para ellos el loco era yo
—Sui Generis, *Las botas locas*

After having lived for almost three years in Israel and Denmark, I returned to Argentina in February of 1979. In June I enlisted in the military service in the Command and Service Company, 3rd Battalion of the Marine Infantry in the woods near La Plata. I went in with the second group of people from the class of 1960, even though I was from the class of 1958, because in 1975 my mom, with her habitual sense of caution, had insisted that I asked to delay my military service until 1979.

Besides learning to use the FAL (light automatic rifle), in the 3rd Battalion (known as the BIM 3) I learned how to operate artillery and PCR377 radio equipment made in Israel. I learned to install antennas to enlarge their frequency amplitudes and to operate radio equipment placed on Volvo trucks, which the military had recently imported from Sweden. In the Marine Infantry I was taught how to disembark from amphibious vehicles. After a long trip to the south in the ARA Cabo San Antonio in late 1979, I participated in simulations and in an exercise at the Naval Base Puerto Belgrano, which lasted ten days, along with the FAPA (Amphibious Support Force).

Exile From Argentina: A Jewish Family and the Military Dictatorship (1976–1983), 2nd Edition, pages 71–82.

We spent most of the time running, cleaning and sweeping. In this book I won't go into detail about the routine and daily life in the service—run, clean, sweep—toward the end of the 1970s because I have little to add to the wonderful descriptions that Guillermo Obiols presents in his book *La memoria del soldado.*

Another activity that I had to participate in while in the BIM 3 was to stand guard at the Astillero Río Santiago, on board of the frigate Santísima Trinidad, which the British were building for the Marines. I remember that I enjoyed this because I could spend the entire week in the shipyard, out of the BIM 3, and besides that I got to eat the same lunch as the workers which, compared to food of the battalion, was incredible. During this time I could also read books and practice my English with the British technicians who were working on the construction of the frigate. But what I liked the most of this were those times I was able to steal some time to myself from the oppressive order that one lived in while in the BIM 3.

I clearly remember that we spent a lot of our break time lying on the grass behind the canteen of the BIM 3, eating alfajores, drinking Coca-Cola and smoking Particulares and Parisiennes. At that time I smoked about two packs of cigarettes a day. In the BIM 3 I was with two guys from La Plata whose lasts names were Arriaga and Luna, and with whom I transferred from the 80 mm Cannon Section to the Communications Section. Many times, we would rest while standing guard and we would share cigarettes and food that we would buy at the canteen or that our parents would bring us.

I also remember Rossi, who worked as the barber. He was the only person in the battalion who had the keys to the salon. With Rossi and other guys—it's hard for me to use the term "marines"—we would spend entire weekends hiding there, smoking and eating. We hid because we were tired and didn't want to be sent to cleaning duty. An interesting fact is that the building where the barber place was located, a few months before I had gotten there, had served as a morgue. It was there that the task force hid the bodies. I remember a noncom that went to get his hair cut there would say, "Up until recently this place still smelled like blood and there were bodies piled up to the ceiling." Back then I thought he was just playing with us, just joking about it. But as I write this, I'm not so sure that those were jokes. During the dictatorship, according to the report by the CONADEP and human rights organizations, the BIM 3 served as a Clandestine Detention Center (CDC) where people were kidnapped, tortured and made to disappear. Amongst them were Hugo Daniel Carzoglio, María Elena Acosta Velasco, Osvaldo Busetto, Ariel Ricetti, Rodolfo Crespo and Carlos Lucero. In the year 2000 the army sold the buildings in which the BIM 3 operated to a private enterprise for the construction of a supermarket. Human rights organizations have declared that in such places one could find remains of the victims of the dictatorship.

At the beginning of my military service, some of the officers and non-coms thought that I was subversive. I remember, as if it were yesterday, that I was interrogated twice. First they set up a table with the Lieutenant R and noncom G, both from Intelligence, in the office of the General Staff. Then they took me for a walk to the depths of the battalion with noncom F, which probably belonged to the internal security battalion. These are the conversations, constructed from my memory which went on between these two men and me:

> *I'm in an office of the General Staff of the BIM 3, sitting on a small bench about a meter away from the table where Lieutenant R and noncom G are seated.*

R: What did you do before joining the infantry?

EDF: I was studying at the University of Jerusalem, in Jerusalem.

G: Do you have any siblings?

EDF: I have three.

G: What do they do?

EDF: My sister Paula is four years old, and my brother Jorge is in high school.

R: You said you had three siblings. Who is the other one?

EDF: Oh, yes. My brother Roberto lives in Israel.

R: What does your brother do in Israel?

EDF: He studies history and German at the Hebrew University of Jerusalem.

R: German, eh? Well, go back to your company now.

EDF: Understood, Lieutenant, sir.

> *I am walking in the depths of the battalion with Corporal F.*

F: Do you have a girlfriend, soldier?

EDF: No, Corporal.

F: You're not gay, are you?

EDF: No, Corporal.

F: Do you do drugs?

EDF: No, Corporal.

   F: Do you like the battalion?

EDF: It's better than being in Puerto Belgrano or in the south.

   F: I don't like the army. I study architecture. I can't wait to be discharged, but they won't do it yet.

EDF: I also prefer to be a civilian, even though I have nothing against a military career.

During my year of military service, I saw some indications that the BIM 3 was participating in the Dirty War. In the communication section the noncoms and the officers would speak loosely about the Task Force's radio equipment about those that required careful maintenance. One day, noncom O, who was in charge of the Communications Section, ordered me to clean the PRC377 Tadiran radio equipment, which was made in Israel. The radio lay on one of the highest shelves of the Wireless Radio Section. While I was cleaning, Corporal N saw me and started yelling furiously, "Faingold! You idiot! Don't touch the *force's* equipment!" This wasn't the only time that I heard one of the noncoms make a reference, either directly or indirectly, to something related the repressive operations executed from the BIM 3. I already mentioned the stories of the bodies of murdered people in the hair salon of the battalion, mentioned by the corporal in passing.

At that time there were also some clues about there being a relationship between the Argentine military and the *tzava* (Israeli army). The radio equipment, fragmentation grenades and other supplies that we used in 1979 and 1980 were made in Israel. Years later, in 1984, when I worked at the reception desk of the Diplomat Hotel in Jerusalem, I told an Israeli who worked security that I had been in the Marine Infantry in Argentina in 1979, to which he responded laughing, "I also did my military service in Argentina at the same time, but training and assessing the Argentine military." This officer told me that he and other soldiers from the Israeli army taught the Argentine soldiers how to use all kinds of weapons and equipment made in Israel. In the book *Israel and Latin America: The Military Connection*, Bishara Bahbah and Linda Butler reveal that Israel was able to penetrate the weapons market in Argentina thanks to the politics and human rights effort of President Carter with this country that prohibited the sales of North American weapons. They also point out that at the same time Argentina's anti-Semitism and the persecution of local Jews was well-known, but Israel's "macho" image allowed that weapons seller to be welcome. This is how in the late 1970s Argentina became Israel's most important buyer of weapons while, ironically, the Argentine military's anti-Semitism was reaching its peak at the same time.

During my military service, I was able to observe this duality of anti-Semitism and admiration for Israel that they had in the military. These are some of the conversations, constructed from my memory that took place between Lieutenant R, the noncoms G and O and me:

> *I'm in formation with the Communications Section in the BIM 3.*

G: I support Hitler. All you Jews should be killed.

EDF: Why?

> *"G" doesn't say anything. He turns around and leaves with an angry expression on his face.*

> *I'm in the Communications Section building a few hours after my confrontation with noncom G.*

O: I heard you had a problem with noncom G.

EDF: It was nothing.

O: Don't act dumb. Next time that someone bothers you about being Jewish, tell me about it immediately. Nobody bothers my soldiers without my permission. That is an order. Understood?

EDF: Understood.

> *I'm with the Communications Section practicing throwing Israeli fragmentation grenades.*

R: No, Faingold, you're not throwing. You already practiced enough when you were in Lebanon (R laughs).

EDF: As you command, Lieutenant, sir.

> *R sees a soldier giving a cookie to another soldier who is standing guard on the roof of the canteen of the BIM 3. I'm on the floor, smoking a cigarette.*

R: (Begins to walk towards the soldier that is eating and to the one that gave him the food.) You two are under arrest for eating while standing guard!

R: (He turns to me) What would they do to these two in the Israeli army?

EDF: In Israel they would cut off their heads at least. (R laughs).

> *I'm with the Communications Section which is already in formation; R organizes the Christmas and New Year's guards.*

> **R:** Faingold, you're going to bring champagne to the soldiers that are standing guard.
>
> **EDF:** And why me?
>
> **R:** Because you guys have money. (R emphasizes "you guys").
>
> **EDF:** Us who?
>
> **R:** You the soldiers. Who else would it be? (R laughs).

While I was in the military I became close friend with Juan, from La Plata. Juan came from a middle class family, the son of Greek immigrants, and graduated from high school from the Colegio Nacional of La Plata in 1976, the same year that I graduated from the Liceo, one of the other high schools that were part of the same University. Just like me, Juan asked to delay his military duty and do it with the class of 1960 in 1979. He was in his third year of college, studying civil engineering when he had to enlist. We met in the barracks of the recruitment center of Marine Infantry (CIFIM), which was located in the woods of the Pereira Iraola Park while we were waiting to be told where we would be assigned. Along with other "slaves" we carried heavy railroad ties that they would use to cook disgusting stews in giant metal pots at the CIFIM.

I remember that one very cold winter morning, while in formation to go to the "ranch," the noncom in charge of the CIFIM asked if anyone spoke English. Juan and I jumped up at the chance to show that we spoke English and other languages. We immediately started teaching him English for a week until we were assigned our destinations, using tapes and an English lesson book that belonged to the officer. At one point, without thinking about it, the officer told us that he had to learn English quickly because the Marine Infantry was sending him to take a course for foreign military personnel that the United Kingdom was giving in Northern Ireland. He told us this as if we knew nothing about what the British troops were doing in Ulster!

That winter, with the second group of the class of 1960, we had three possible locations to go to in the Marine Infantry: the BIM 3 (in the woods of La Plata), the Navy Base of Puerto Belgrano (close to Bahía Blanca), and the worst, the BIM 5 (in Tierra del Fuego). For Juan and I there was only one possible destination. Because of our connections, we were "placed" in the BIM 3, a few blocks from our houses. Juan was placed there because of an admiral who was a friend of the family. I was placed there because my dad's mechanic also fixed the cars of many of the military men in the area of La Plata. During the first few weeks in the navy, we were in the same section of the Command and Services Company, Cannons 80 mm, but we were soon reassigned. Juan was sent to the Justice Section of the General Staff and I was sent first to the Mortar Section, and then to the Communications Sections, of the same company, Command and Services.

In a conversation with Juan (La Plata 10/29/03), he tells me about what happened during his military service:

EDF: How did you end up in the BIM 3?

J: The same way that I ended up in the Marine Infantry. The BIM 3 was close to the university so I could continue studying. I would leave early, sometimes at noon, sometimes at two, and I was comfortable with that.

EDF: Do you have any interesting stories about your time in the army?

J: There are many. Do you remember when they almost killed me? Do you remember that in cannons there was an officer that was a paratrooper? A tall guy? One day, I don't know why, he had a thug hit me on the head with a metal bar and they had to take me to the Naval Hospital. The thing was, I had permission to leave early and the head of the company, Lieutenant [RL], told me that it was no longer valid. He didn't let me leave. They put [RL] under arrest because of me. The guy could have killed me; I didn't die because I got lucky. He sent some soldiers when I was sleeping, they hit me on the head with a metal bar and I was taken to the Naval Hospital. They gave me stitches for that. They could have killed me. This officer came to talk to me, a proper man, so I wouldn't cause a scene. My dad wanted to turn them in.

EDF: Couldn't they have made your dad disappear?

J: No. They knew that with my connections they couldn't make me disappear. But everything ended there and since then [RL] never really talked to me again.

EDF: Do you think that noncom [G], Lieutenant [R] and the commander were part of the secret task force?

J: [R] and [G] were for sure. It was the one that was next to the officers club. That building that was there and there were some other ones. The thing is that there were other military men who didn't appear as part of the battalion. They apparently dressed as civilians who came and went in the night. The thing is, is that they all went through Justice and everybody's files were there. There was a Captain [V] who belonged to the force. I don't think he was part of the battalion but he had his operation branch in the battalion. There were also vehicles that belonged to the task forces. They were parked. They were cars like Ford Falcons, civilian vehicles. They were parked in auto garages, but they were also parked where the force was, behind the officers club. But none of this was ever talked about. There was a sort of subliminal message. Everybody knew, but no one talked about it. I think that the secret task force had its headquarters in the General Staff and that the majority of the battalion didn't participate in it.

EDF: And who were the soldiers that were with you at the General Staff offices?

J: It was a whole group of people that were related to the military. Somebody had recommended them there, somebody with power. An admiral recommended me there, I don't remember his name. They knew that I was someone they could trust. Just think that I had my hands on all the justice files that were part of the General Staff offices. I knew that, "this guy is in jail, [R] is in jail."

EDF: And who were the other soldiers?

J: They were friends with some officer, like Bravo was. Do you remember Bravo? He had been classmates with some officer, with the one in charge of the offices. That one wasn't part of the force. His name was . . . I don't remember. He was a very good person. He left the Marines after that.

EDF: How could you tell if someone was involved in the task forces or not?

J: Because there were subliminal threats. Do you remember that they used to say, "Watch out, because you're going to be in combat, which way are you going to fire your rifles? Don't be stupid"! [R], [G], and that corporal who was an architect; they were in the secret task force. That architect was in the force as a spy, to see if anyone said certain things.

EDF: Did he take you for a walk?

J: Yes, he was the kind of guy that could tell. From those walks some people never came back. He was a snitch. It was his job in the battalion and in the university. They would send him to the university to study. They would send him on those well-known "walks." But he didn't take just anyone. He took us. We were potential enemies. If we came back from those walks we had security clearance. He was a normal noncom, but it seems that he wasn't a normal noncom. Maybe he wasn't a noncom, maybe he was being punished.

He was part of the force, probably in the internal security department. He was there just in case that there was someone suspicious, to make him disappear. He always made comments against the military, to see if you would take the bait. He took me on one of those walks too. And then they would get rid of people there. He said that subversives, their children, their families and their grandparents should be killed. He would wait to see our reactions. He said it to see if someone would respond. Obviously no one said anything. Another one that was for sure in the force was the noncom to whom we taught English. He was a torturer and he would admit it to your face. He had been in Northern Ireland. I don't remember his name. That's why he wanted to learn English. And that guy was definitely part of it.

EDF: Did you see anything odd or suspicious when you were in the Justice section, in the General Staff offices?

J: No, all of that took place at night. We used to leave at two in the afternoon or five at the latest. The ones who were standing guard may have seen something. They could have seen the cars leave.

EDF: Did you ever have a run-in with noncom [G]?

J: Not that I remember. But there were always problems with guys who had some level of education. There were few of those. Most of the people there didn't really study. He knew that we didn't like him. That's why there were always veiled threats. Even with simple things like telling us that we didn't get the day off or that we couldn't go out. I think he was a natural torturer. He enjoyed torturing people because he was a coward. Just like [R], when he had to fight the British, he gave up. I saw in a film that they were coming back from the Georgias, and there was [R]. He was one of the Lizards. He had given up, as one would expect. He was good at torturing, but not good in combat.

EDF: So he was a powerful man?

J: Yes, but there were people above him. The Chief of Operations, whose name I don't remember. He was a G1 or G2, which was the third officer in rank. Communications was some sort of annex for him, that's why he had noncom [O] who was an able guy and managed communications, and in intelligence he had [G]. [G] was the one that worked for [R]. No one went in to [G]'s office, it was only him. [G] had many problems with the people in the General Staff. Nobody liked him. He had a degree of alienation because of the torturing; he didn't realize when he was disrespectful to an officer and more than once he ended up getting arrested. Just like [R] every once in a while he would get arrested.

EDF: The officers from artillery weren't part of it?

J: No, they were taught about it, but they didn't participate. Those three definitely were, but I never saw captain [V].

EDF: And how do you know he existed?

J: Because the people in justice knew him. The guy was sometimes here, and sometimes he went somewhere else. I never saw him in person, only on paper. Evidently a person who was in the force ended up being in a different jurisdiction. There were receipts of salaries, but I don't know if [V] was really his name. He had also been processed for some administrative fault and he passed through justice as a battalion member. But it was known that he was part of the battalion because someone was getting that salary.

EDF: What soldiers were with you in the General Staff offices?

J: [R] chose intelligent men to assist him. Like that guy Nimo, the son of the sports telecaster, and Bauer, one of Conrado Bauer's sons, who was a minister during the dictatorship. In intelligence there weren't any soldiers. It was only [R] and [G]. They would ask us people in justice for favors and things.

EDF: Any other story?

J: Do you remember when we were in the arena at the CIFIM with those ponchos made of blankets? We looked like prisoners of war. I remember that arena, that's where we met. There was quite a crowd there. We didn't deal with any officers there. I remember when the noncom in charge told us that he was going to Ireland, as if no one knew what was going on in Northern Ireland. They didn't think that we were knowledgeable enough to know what they were talking about. They couldn't talk to their peers. They would have put them in prison. We were like a free psychologist to him. You were the perfect psychologist because you weren't going to say anything.

EDF: Like the prisoners in the ESMA?

J: Yes, like the prisoners in the ESMA. In a way, yes.

EDF: Do you find that it was a good thing to have experienced these things in the military?

J: In a way, yes. What happened was that many people went through those same places and never realized what was going on; that's the big issue. The majority of the people that were there didn't know anything about the situation. They didn't know what the task force was or what [R] or anyone else did. All of this has to be put in the perspective of those times; many people didn't know what was going on. The thing is that we saw all of that from the inside, because we knew what was going on. Someone who went in not knowing what was going on wouldn't see anything. What was noticeable was that everyone knew that they had cars that had been stolen. There were stolen cars that were registered in their names. Just like when one occupies an enemy country, they acted like they were doing these things to their enemies, not their own kind. They would take television sets and electrical appliances. In General Staff they would talk about how this or that person had won something in a lawsuit. They would say it as a joke. Apparently, during the roughest time, before we got there, they would bring back a lot of things to the battalion. The people from the forces would take things and then divide them up amongst themselves.

Finally, in April of 1980, on a cold day but with a winter sun shining down, I was finally discharged from the Marine Infantry. I handed back the much-hated TIN (Naval Identification Card) and they gave me back my Documento Nacional de Identidad (DNI, National Identity Card). With my DNI in hand, I was back to being a civilian.

During my time in the service, I had a lot of time to think about the choice that I had made in February of 1979 while in Denmark, to return to Argentina. I never regretted coming back to fulfill my military service. Without a passport, they would have recruited me into the army for three years in Israel and in Denmark I would have been a refugee without citizenship anywhere, always at the mercy of the bureaucrats of the Danish government.

When I was discharged from the Marine Infantry, I could no longer see myself living in the Argentina of 1980, nor studying at the university there that had been infiltrated by the military, nor working in a country that was permanently in a coup d'etat, in which the forces of the military oppression operated with impunity and people were still disappearing. With the DNI in my hand, I could renew my passport and go wherever I wanted to go. I played around with the idea of returning to Israel or Europe in my mind. At that time, I also saw South Africa as a possibility where I could use my knowledge of Spanish and English to work with the Argentine tourism industry which, in the early 1980s, was strong. Argentines would travel in big groups thanks to the strength of the peso, which we called "sweet money." I made my final decision to leave because of an unexpected event that took place two weeks after I left the Marine Infantry. One day I went to see a late night movie at the theater on Lavalle Street in Buenos Aires to see *Apocalypse Now*, directed by Francis Ford Coppola in 1979, which was about Vietnam. At around three in the morning, I was a few blocks away from my aunt Teresa's house where I was going to spend the night. While walking down Rivadavia Avenue, close to Nazca Street, two police officers stopped me. First they had me against a wall with my hands in the air for over half an hour while they asked me what I was doing out on the street at that time of night. Finally, they let me put my hands down, but they still had me facing the wall until I pointed out to them that there was a stamp on my DNI that showed I had recently been discharged from the Marine Infantry. I told them that up until recently, as my document stated, I had been a member of the Armed Forces. I remember clearly that I wasn't afraid, but instead merely annoyed. I probably felt disgusted because I had just gotten out of the military service in which for a year the noncoms and officers had treated me as they wished morning, day and night. After almost three hours of waiting on the street against a wall, at around six in the morning, a trooper finally arrived with a computer that had the police's data registry of the inhabitants of the city. The agents gave my DNI to the officer that was in the car. After seeing my last name he asked me if I had relatives in the police force. I told him yes, that my cousins Carlos and Ernesto Faingold, my uncle Naúm's sons, were *comisarios* (sheriffs) of the Police of the Province of Buenos Aires. Immediately, the police officer in the patrol car gave the order for them to let me go. The run-in with the cops was the last straw. In those times, I realized that I lived in a country in which one couldn't go out in the streets without being harassed by the oppressive forces of the dictatorship; a country in which the night, clearly, belonged to the police and to the military. That same week I renewed my passport, and shortly afterwards I returned to Israel.

Epilogue

Where in hell can you go far from the things that you know
Far from the sprawl of concrete that keeps crawling its way about 1,000 miles a day
Take one last look behind, commit this to memory and mind
Don't miss this wasteland, this terrible place
When you leave keep your heart off your sleeve

—Natalie Merchant, *Motherland*

In May of 1980 I returned to Israel. A few days after arriving I got a job working at the pool at the Hilton in Jerusalem. Between my salary and tips I made a lot of money. I spent most of it on beer at the Tavern bar, which was downtown, and buying rock cassette tapes. At that time I got accepted to the College of Humanities in the University of Jerusalem. At my brother Roberto's house I met Sonia, one of the most beautiful and intelligent women that I have ever met, and I fell in love with her at first sight. Sonia was born in São Paulo and had lived in Israel since she was thirteen. We got married eight months after we met. As I write this book, Sonia and I are celebrating our 25th anniversary and have just returned from our second honeymoon in Europe.

Before we got married we lived in an apartment on the corner of Yaffo and King George, right in the middle of downtown Jerusalem that we shared with Marcos Resnitzky, whom I have already mentioned. Around that time Sonia was beginning her doctorate in neurobiology and I was beginning my first year majoring in English linguistics and French language and

Exile From Argentina: A Jewish Family and the Military Dictatorship (1976–1983), 2nd Edition, pages 83–84.

literature. Marcos was studying chemistry, even though his true calling was law and politics.

In 1984 I received my diploma in English linguistics and French language and literature (BA). That same year my son Noam was born. In 1987 I finished my master's degree (MA) in English linguistics. I received both degrees from the Hebrew University in Jerusalem. In 1993 I got my doctorate (PhD) in general linguistics from the University of Tel-Aviv. Later I did research at the University of California in Los Angeles between 1990 and 1992 and I taught classes in Spanish at the State University of New York at Stony Brook between 1992 and 1995. Since 1995 I have been teaching linguistics and film classes and have been a researcher at the University of Tulsa in Oklahoma, where I live with Sonia and Noam.

Nowadays my parents live in La Plata, after three failed attempts to move to Israel in 1970, 1980 and 1990. Roberto lives in Brazil with his wife Annette and his children Alon and Nurit. Jorge lives in Norway with his wife Eva and his daughters Sib, Sabina and Amanda. Paula lives in Israel with her husband Amir and their sons Liam and Noam. We are four siblings that live in four different countries. It is interesting that Sonia and her sisters also live in different countries: Brazil, U.S., England and Israel.

In this book, I will not go into further detail about my family; a family that has its roots in five countries, where we live with five different cultures, and where we speak various languages. The subject of my "transnational" family will be saved for my next memoir. Meanwhile, in my book *Multilingualism from Infancy to Adolescence: Noam's Experience*, the curious reader can find some information about my life with Sonia and Noam in Israel in the 1980s and in the U.S. in the 1990s.

Questionnaire 1

Los que se Quedaron

1. ¿Cuántos años tenés?
2. Contame un poco de tu familia, de tu infancia, ¿Cómo estaba compuesta tu familia?
3. ¿Cómo viviste la época anterior al golpe?
4. ¿Cómo fueron tus estudios hasta la dictadura?
   ¿Militabas?
   ¿Tenías miedo?
   ¿Hubo alguna señal en el colegio o en la facultad que te permitiera prever lo que luego pasó?
5. ¿Qué hacías en 1976?
   ¿Estudiabas o trabajabas?
   ¿A qué colegio o facultad ibas?
   ¿Dónde trabajabas?
   ¿Qué edad tenías?
   Contame un poco de tus experiencias ese año.
6. ¿Te allanaron la casa a vos o a algún familiar o amigo cercano?
   ¿Tenés familiares o amigos desaparecidos?

Questionnaire 2

Los que se Fueron

1. ¿Cuántos años tenés?
2. Contame un poco de tu familia, de tu infancia, ¿Cómo estaba compuesta tu familia?
3. ¿Cómo viviste la época anterior al golpe?
4. ¿Cómo fueron tus estudios hasta la dictadura?
   ¿Militabas?
   ¿Tenías miedo?
   ¿Hubo alguna señal en el colegio o en la facultad que te permitiera prever lo que luego pasó?
5. ¿Qué hacías en 1976?
   ¿Estudiabas o trabajabas?
   ¿A qué colegio o facultad ibas?
   ¿Dónde trabajabas?
   ¿Qué edad tenías?
   Contame un poco de tus experiencias ese año.
6. ¿Te allanaron la casa a vos o a algún familiar o amigo cercano?
   ¿Tenés familiares o amigos desaparecidos?
7. ¿Te tuviste que ir de tu ciudad o del país?
8. ¿Cuántos años tenías cuando te fuiste?
9. ¿En qué punto de tus estudios estabas cuando tuviste que irte?
10. ¿Quién tomó la decisión de irse del país?
11. ¿Emigró toda tu familia?
    ¿Se fueron juntos?
12. ¿Cómo fue el momento de la partida?

13. ¿Habías viajado anteriormente?
14. ¿Cuáles fueron las mayores pérdidas que tuviste al irte de Argentina?
15. ¿A qué país(es) te fuiste?
    ¿Trabajaste?
    ¿Estudiaste?
16. ¿Aprendiste otros idiomas?
    ¿Adquiriste una residencia o ciudadanía extranjera?
    ¿Fue fácil?
    ¿Cómo te mantenías económicamente?
17. ¿Cómo era la comunicación con los que se quedaron?
    ¿Te escribías?
    ¿Con quién?
    ¿Viajabas a encontrarte con familiares y/o amigos?
    ¿Te venían a visitar?
18. ¿Intentaste volver?
    Contame sobre esas experiencias.
19. ¿Sentías la sensación de crecer o, por el contrario, una especie de involución?
20 ¿Hoy en día cómo te sentís?
21. ¿Cómo es tu relación con Argentina apartir de tu experiencia de exilio?
    ¿Te sentís más parte del país o menos?
22. ¿Qué te ha dejado el exilio?
    Una reflexión final sobre el exilio.

Paternal Roots: Faingold

1.

Marcos Faingold
[m. Neja Shein, 1]
[m. Berta Rosenbaum, 2]

2.

Children of Marcos Faingold with Neja Shein

Syvie Faingold

Paulina Faingold
[m. Ramírez]

Raquel Faingold
[m. Paulina Teper]

Abraham Faingold

Children of Marcos Faingold with Berta Rosenbaum

Isaac Faingold

José Faingold

Miguel Faingold

Samuel Faingold

Gerardo Faingold

Ester Faingold

Julia Faingold

Elena Faingold

Sara Faingold

Flora Faingold

Children of Berta Rosenbaum, Stepchildren of Marcos Faingold

Israel (Teper) Faingold
[m. Raquel Zimerman]

Paulina Teper
[m. Abraham Faingold]

Exile From Argentina: A Jewish Family and the Military Dictatorship (1976–1983), 2nd Edition, pages 89–92.
Copyright © 2024 by Information Age Publishing
www.infoagepub.com

3.

Children of Abraham Faingold

Naúm Faingold
[m. Salvadora Álvarez]

Teresa Faingold
[m. Mauricio Korbenfeld]

Natalia Faingold
(m. Jaime Vinderman]

Enrique Faingold
[m. Annie Faingold]

Children of Israel Faingold

Natalio Faingold
[m. Luz]

Rosita Faingold
[m. Felipe Alberto Villagra]

Julita Faingold
[m. Hugo Fernández Artucio]

4.

Children of Naúm Faingold

Ernesto Faingold

Carlos Faingold

Children of Teresa Faingold de Korbenfeld

Puli Korbenfeld
[m. Jorge Berendorf, 1]
[m. José Burucúa, 2]

Hector Korbenfeld
[m. Rosa Nacach]

Children of Natalia Faingold de Vinderman

Paulinita Vinderman
[m. Marcelo Burstein, 1]
[m. Jorge Cabrera, 2]

Children of Enrique Faingold

Roberto Faingold
[m. Anet Zimerman]

Eduardo Faingold
[m. Sonia Hocherman]

Jorge Faingold
[m. Eva Schwartz]

Paula Faingold
[m. Amir Elion]

Children of Natalio Faingold

Natalio Faingold

Luz Faingold

Marcos Faingold

Children of Rosita Faingold de Villagra

Helena Villagra
[m. Mario Mactas, 1]
[m. Rodolfo Ortega Peña, 2]
[m. Eduardo Galeano, 3]

Lily Villagra

Raquel Villagra

Elsa Villagra

Child of Julita Faingold de Fernández Artucio (Uruguay)

Hugo Fernández Faingold
[m. Ana María]

Nephews of Rosita Faingold de Villagra

Nelda Villagra
[m. Lito Lebensohn]

Agustín Villagra

5.

Children of Puli Korbenfeld

Andrés Berendorf
[m. Daniela Alterman]

Diego Berendorf
[m. María Dolores Martínez]

Children of Hector Korbenfeld

Ernesto Korbenfeld
[m. Elisa Vitkot]

Daniela Korbenfeld
[m. Daniel Caride]

Child of Paulinita Vinderman

Mariel Burstein

Children of Roberto Faingold (Brazil)

Alon Faingold

Nurit Faingold

Child of Eduardo Faingold (United States)

Noam Faingold

Children of Jorge Faingold (Norway)

Sieb Faingold

Sabina Faingold

Amanda Faingold

Children of Paula Faingold de Elion (Israel)

Liam Elion   Noam Elion

Child of Helena Villagra

Mariana Mactas

Maternal Roots: Turkenich

$\overline{1.}$

Naftuli Turkenich
[m. Dina Gulman]

$\overline{2.}$

Children of Naftuli Turkenich

Roberto Turkenich
[m. Lía Mindlin]

Batsheva Turkenich

[?]

Rosa Turkenich
[m. Abraham Kort]

Zelik Turkenich
[m. Ana Volpin]

[?]

$\overline{3.}$

Children of Rosa Turkenich de Kort

Marcos Kort

Natalia Kort

Moshe Kort

Gregorio Kort

Children of Zelik Turkenich

Annie Turkenich
[m. Enrique Faingold]

Isaac Turkenich
[m. Victoria Cohen]

Exile From Argentina: A Jewish Family and the Military Dictatorship (1976–1983), 2nd Edition, pages 93–94.
Copyright © 2024 by Information Age Publishing
www.infoagepub.com

4.

Children of Annie Turkenich de Faingold

Roberto Faingold
[m. Anet Zimerman]

Eduardo Faingold
[m. Sonia Hocherman]

Jorge Faingold
[m. Eva Schwartz]

Paula Faingold
[m. Amir Elion]

Children of Isaac Turkenich

Daniel Turkenich

5.

Children of Roberto Faingold (Brazil)

Alon Faingold

Nurit Faingold

Child of Eduardo Faingold (United States)

Noam Faingold

Children of Jorge Faingold (Norway)

Sieb Faingold

Sabina Faingold

Amanda Faingold

Children of Paula Faingold de Elion (Israel)

Liam Elion

Noam Elion

Maternal Roots: Volpin and Teplitz

1.

Mairim Teplitz
[m. ?]

2.

[?] Volpin
[m. ?]

Jaim Isaac Teplitz
[m. Ester Nieshe Berman]

3.

Children of [?] *Volpin*

Shame Volpin

José Volpin

[?]

Samuel Volpin
[m. Mashe Teplitz]

Marcos Volpin
[m. Rifka]

[?]

*Exile From Argentina: A Jewish Family and the Military
Dictatorship (1976–1983), 2nd Edition*, pages 95–97.
Copyright © 2024 by Information Age Publishing
www.infoagepub.com
All rights of reproduction in any form reserved.

Children of Jaim Isaac Teplitz

Abraham Teplitz

Mairim Teplitz

Mashe Teplitz
[m. Samuel Volpin]

Jaike Teplitz

Inde Teplitz

Meite Teplitz

Leiche Teplitz

4.

Children of Samuel Volpin

Ana Volpin
[m. Zelik Turkenich]

Raquel Volpin
[m. Isaac Miropolsky]

Marcos Volpin
[m. Rosita]

David Volpin

Maike Volpin
[m. Rebeca Piflacs]

Children of Mairim Teplitz

Simón Teplitz

Abraham Teplitz

Ernesto Teplitz

Marcos Teplitz

5.

Children of Marcos Volpin

Manuel Volpin

David Volpin

Child of Maike Volpin

Samuel Volpin

Children of Ana Volpin de Turkenich

Annie Turkenich
[m. Enrique Faingold]

Isaac Turkenich
[m. Victoria Cohen]

Children of Raquel Volpin de Miropolsky

Amalia Miropolsky
[m. Jorge Minoli]

Ester Miropolsky
[m. Edgardo Yivoff]

Children of Marcos Teplitz

Néstor Teplitz   Estela Nora Teplitz

6.

Children of Annie Turkenich de Faingold

Roberto Faingold   Eduardo Faingold
[m. Anet Zimerman]   [m. Sonia Hocherman]

Jorge Faingold   Paula Faingold
[m. Eva Schwartz]   [m. Amir Elion]

Child of Isaac Turkenich

Daniel Turkenich

Children of Ester Miropolsky

Gustavo Yivoff   Raquel Yivoff

7.

Children of Roberto Faingold (Brazil)

Alon Faingold   Nurit Faingold

Child of Eduardo Faingold (United States)

Noam Faingold

Children of Jorge Faingold (Norway)

Sieb Faingold   Sabina Faingold

Amanda Faingold

Children of Paula Faingold de Elion (Israel)

Liam Elion   Noam Elion

Appendix: Family Photos and Documents

Abraham, Enrique, Teresa, and Natalia Faingold with baby Jorge Faingold in City Bell early 1960s, left to right

Ana Volpin in Medanos early 1940s

Exile From Argentina: A Jewish Family and the Military Dictatorship (1976–1983), 2nd Edition, pages 99–115.
Copyright © 2024 by Information Age Publishing
www.infoagepub.com

Annie Turkenich with her
grandparents Samuel Volpin
and Mashe Teplitz in Medanos
early 1930s

Annie Turkenich with her
parents Zelik and Ana in La
Plata 1935

Berta Rosenbaum early 1900s

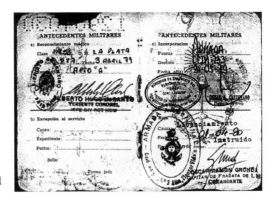

Eduardo Faingold Argentina
ID with military induction and
discharge dates

Eduardo Faingold Bialik Jewish
high school diploma 1976

Enrique Faingold
Genia R. Turkenich de Faingold

tienen el agrade de invitar a Ud. y familia
a la ceremonia religiosa del
Bar Mitzva de su hijo
Eduardo Daniel

que se efectuará el día Sábado 11 de Septiembre,
a las 10 horas en el Templo de la C. M. J. C.
calle 4 N°. 978.

La Plata, Septiembre de 1971

Eduardo Faingold invitation to
bar mitzva in La Plata 1971

Zelik Turkenich Polish Passport
with immigration stamp 1923

Zelik Turkenich Polish Passport with Argentine seal 1920s

Zelik Turkenich and Ana Volpin ketubah 1935

Eduardo Faingold and Jorge Faingold in La Plata 1980

Eduardo Faingold and Paula Faingold in La Plata 1980

Eduardo Faingold and Roberto Faingold at the Hebrew University in Mount Scopus, Jerusalem 1977

Eduardo Faingold and Sonia Hocherman wedding in Ramat Gan 1981

Eduardo Faingold and Sonia Hocherman, Roberto Faingold and Anete Zimerman, and Jorge Faingold at the wedding in Ramat Gan 1981

Eduardo Faingold at the Israel-
Lebanon border 1978

Eduardo Faingold at the Western Wall in Jerusalem 1977

Eduardo Faingold during military maneuvers with BIM3 in
the South Atlantic 1979

Eduardo Faingold during military maneuvers with the Communications Section
of the BIM3 in Puerto Belgrano 1979, third row, second right

Eduardo Faingold in Esbjerg,
Denmark 1978

Eduardo Faingold in La Plata,
1980

Eduardo Faingold in Kibbutz
Kfar Blum 1977

Eduardo Faingold leaving
Argentina 1976

Eduardo Faingold on leave
from BIM3 with Paula Faingold
in Miramar 1980

Eduardo Faingold with Bernadette and Laurie in kibbutz Kfar Blum 1977

Eduardo Faingold with Liceo classmates in La Plata 1976, second right lower row

Eduardo Faingold, Annie,
Roberto and Jorge Faingold in
Buenos Aires early 1960s, right

Enrique Faingold and Annie
Turkenich 1956

Enrique Faingold in Roberts
early 1940s

Enrique Faingold, Annie
Turkenich, Paula Faingold,
baby Nurit and Noam Faingold
in Jerusalem 1987

Jaim and Ester Teplitz in Medanos early 1900s

Marcos Faingold in Algarrobos
early 1900s

Marcos Faingold's sons and daughters with NejaShein and Berta Rosenbaum at a
family reunion in Buenos Aires 1950s

Mashe Teplitz with grandchildren in Medanos late 1940s

Naftuli Turkenich and Dina
Gulman in Russia early 1900s

Neja Shein early 1900s

Sonia Hocherman and Noam
Faingold in East Talpiot Jerusalem 1987

Sonia Hocherman and Noam
Faingold in Jerusalem 1989

Sonia Hocherman and Noam
Faingold in the Roman amphi-
theatre of Beit Shean 1987

Teplitz family in Medanos early
1900s

Volpin family in Medanos early 1900s

Zelik Turkenich and Ana
Turkenich 1934

Zelik Turkenich as hazzan lead-
ing prayers in La Plata early
1990s

Zelik Turkenich at the Swift
meat packing in Berisso, 1930

Zelik Turkenich fresh off the
boat from Poland 1923, left

Zelik Turkenich in Medanos
early 1940s

Zelik Turkenich with his comrades in Poland early 1920s, second left

Sources

Articles and Books

Adam, A. M., Cavilliotti, M., & Gonzalez, O. P. (1997). *Ortega Peña. Un diputado.* Buenos Aires: Paradigma Editores.

Alperson, M. (1922/1991). *Colonia Mauricio. Memoria de un colono judío.* Carlos Casares: Centro Cultural José Ingenieros.

Anguita, E., & Caparrós, M. (1997). *La voluntad. Una historia de la militancia revolucionaria en la Argentina.* Buenos Aires: Grupo Editorial Norma.

Armada Argentina. (1987). *Infantería de Marina.* Buenos Aires: SS & CC Ediciones.

Bahbah, B., & Butler, L. (1986). *Israel and Latin America. The military connection.* New York: St. Martin Press.

Barjavel, R. (1972). *Los caminos a Katmandú.* Buenos Aires: Emecé.

Baron, A., Del Carril, M., & Gómez, A. (1995). *Por qué se fueron. Testimonios de argentinos en el exterior.* Buenos Aires: Emecé.

Bernetti, J. L., & Giardinelli, M. (2003). *México: El exilio que hemos vivido. Memorias del exilio argentino durante la dictadura 1976–1983.* Buenos Aires: Universidad Nacional de Quilmes.

Brocato, C. A. (1986). *Exilio es el nuestro.* Buenos Aires: Sudamericana/Planeta.

Calloni, S. (1999). *Los años del lobo. Operación Cóndor.* Buenos Aires: Ediciones Continente, 2ª edición.

Calveiro, P. (1995). *Poder y desaparición. Los campos de concentración en Argentina.* Buenos Aires: Colihue.

CONADEP. (1984). *Nunca más. Informe de la Comisión Nacional sobre la Desaparición de las Personas.* Buenos Aires: EUDEBA.

Cooper, D. (1972). *La muerte de la familia.* Buenos Aires: Paidós.

Exile From Argentina: A Jewish Family and the Military Dictatorship (1976–1983), 2nd Edition, pages 117–121.
Copyright © 2024 by Information Age Publishing
www.infoagepub.com
All rights of reproduction in any form reserved.

Corbatta, J. (1999). *Narrativas de la guerra sucia en Argentina*. Buenos Aires: Corregidor.

D'Andrea Mohr, J. L. (1998). *El escuadrón perdido*. Buenos Aires: Editorial Planeta.

D'Andrea Mohr, J. L. (1999). *Memoria debida*. Buenos Aires: Colihue.

De Ortube, M. L. (2001). *Nuestro Liceo*. La Plata: Ferrograf.

Dinges, J. (2004). *The Condor years. How Pinochet and the allies brought terrorism to three continents*. New York: The New Press.

Dussel, I., Finocchio, S., & Gojman, S. (2003). *Haciendo memoria en el país de nunca más*. Buenos Aires: Eudeba.

Errecaborde, J. A. (1997). *Anecdotario de la Infantería de Marina de la Armada Argentina*, Buenos Aires: Instituto de Publicaciones Navales.

Evangelista, L. (1998). *Voices of the survivors. Testimony, mourning and memory in post-dictatorship Argentina (1983–1995)*. New York: Garland.

Faingold, E. (2004). *Multilingualism from infancy to adolescence. Noam's experience*. Westport, CT: Information Age.

Feierstein, R. (1999) *Historia de los judíos argentinos*. Buenos Aires: Ameghino.

Fernández Artucio, H. (1940) *Nazis en el Uruguay*. Montevideo: Editorial Sur.

Fernández Artucio, H. (1941). *El proceso a Hugo Fernández Artucio*. Montevideo: Imprenta Letras.

Fernández Faingold, H., Asiaín, R., & Flores Silva, M. (1987). *Colorados*. Montevideo: Monte Sexto.

Galeano, E. (1971/2003). *Las venas abiertas de América Latina*. Madrid: Siglo XXI Editores de España.

Galeano, E. (1984). *Días y noches de amor y de guerra*. Buenos Aires: Catálogos.

Galeano, E. (2004). *Bocas del tiempo*. Buenos Aires: Catálogos.

Gelman, J., & La Madrid, M. (1997). *Ni el flaco perdón de Dios. Hijos de desaparecidos*. Buenos Aires: Planeta.

Gelman, J. & Bayer, O. (1984). *Exilio*. Buenos Aires: Editorial Legasa.

Geraños, S. & Pertot, W. (2002) *La otra Juvenilia. Militancia y represión en el Colegio Nacional Buenos Aires 1971–1986*. Buenos Aires: Editorial Biblos.

Goloboff, M. (2002). *The Algarrobos quartet*. Albuquerque: University of New Mexico Press.

Gorriarán Merlo, E. (2003). *Memorias de Enrique Gorriarán Merlo. De los setenta a la Tablada*. Buenos Aires: Planeta.

Graham-Yooll, A. (1999). *Memoria del miedo*. Buenos Aires: Editorial de Belgrano.

Groppo, B., & Flier, P., (Eds.) (2001). *La imposibilidad del olvido. Recuerdos de la memoria en Argentina, Chile y Uruguay*. La Plata: Ediciones Al Margen.

Guelar, D., Jarach, V., & Ruiz, B. (2002). *Los chicos del exilio*. Buenos Aires: El País de Nomeolvides.

Herman, D. L. (1984). *The Latin American community of Israel*. New York: Praeger.

Hess, M. (1958). *Rome and Jerusalem*. New York: Philosophical Library.

Jensen, S. (2004). Política y cultura del exilio en Cataluña. In P. Yankelevich (Ed.), *Represión y destierro. Itinerarios del exilio argentino.* La Plata: Ediciones Al Margen.

Josephs, R. (1944). *Argentine diary.* New York: Random House.

Lewis, P. (2002). *Guerrillas and generals. The Dirty War in Argentina.* Westport, CT: Praeger.

Laing, R. D. (1973). *Nudos.* Buenos Aires: Sudamericana.

Lvovich, D. (2003). *Nacionalismo y antisemitismo en la Argentina.* Buenos Aires: Javier Bergara.

Mittleberg, D. (1988). *Strangers in paradise. The Israeli kibbutz experience.* New York: Transaction Books.

Mort, J., & Brenner, G. (2003). *Our hearts invented the place.* Ithaca, NY: Cornell University Press.

Natenberg, T. (2002) *The journey within. Two months on kibbutz.* Chicago: Writers Club.

Obiols, G. (2003). *La memoria del soldado. Campo de Mayo (1976–1977).* Buenos Aires: Eudeba.

Parcero, D., Helfgot, M., & Dulce, D. (1985). *La Argentina exiliada.* Buenos Aires: Centro Editor de América Latina.

Politzer, G. (1961). *Principios elementales y fundamentales de filosofía.* Buenos Aires: Hemisferios.

Pujol, S. (2002). *La década rebelde. Los años 60 en la Argentina.* Buenos Aires: Emecé.

Quién es quién en La Plata. (1972). La Plata: Cáritas.

Rein, R. (2001). *Argentina, Israel y los judíos. Encuentros y desencuentros, mitos y realidades.* Buenos Aires: Ediciones Lumière.

Schoultz, L. (1981). *Human rights and the United States Policy towards Latin America.* Princeton, NJ: Princeton University Press.

Seoane, M., & Ruiz Nuñez, H. (2003). *La noche de los lápices.* Buenos Aires: Editorial Sudamericana.

Sheinin, D., & Baer Barr, L., (Eds.) (1996). *The Jewish diaspora in Latin America. New studies in history and literature.* New York: Garland.

Sznajder, M., & Roniger, L. (2004). De Argentina a Israel: Escape y exilio. In P. Yankelevich (Ed.), *Represión y destierro. Itinerarios del exilio argentino.* La Plata: Ediciones Al Margen.

Timerman, J. (1982). *Prisoner without a name, cell without a number.* New York: Vintage.

Ulanovsky, C. (2001). *Seamos felices mientras estamos aquí. Crónicas de exilio.* Buenos Aires: Editorial Sudamericana.

Weisbrot, R. (1979). *The Jews of Argentina. From the inquisition to Perón.* Philadelphia: The Jewish Publication Society of America.

Yankelevich, P. (2004). Tras las huellas del exilio. In P. Yankelevich (Ed.), *Represión y destierro. Itinerarios del exilio argentino.* La Plata: Ediciones Al Margen.

Zimerman de Faingold, R. (1981). *Memorias.* Buenos Aires: Publicación Privada.

Zito Lema, V. (1978). *Homenaje a Rodolfo Ortega Peña.* Barcelona: Agermanament.
Zuker, C. (2003). *El tren de la victoria. Una saga familiar.* Buenos Aires: Editorial Sudamericana.

Newspapers

El Día (La Plata)
Clarín (Buenos Aires)
Haaretz
La Nación (Buenos Aires)
La Nueva Provincia
Le Monde
The New York Times
Página 12

Web Pages

www.apdhlaplata.org.ar

www.belarusguide.com

www.comunidadboliviana.com

www.ensenada.gov.ar

www.generacionesmv.com

www.goalweb.com/world/kfarblum.html

www.jewishgen.org

www.goalweb.com/world/kfarblum.htm

Interviews

Amalia Miropolsky de Minoli (cousin of the author's mother)

Annie Turkenich de Faingold (author's mother)

Armando (author's friend)

Cecilia (author's friend)

Elsita (author's friend)

Juan (author's friend)

Julia Faingold de Fernández Artucio (cousin of the author's father)

Mónica (author's friend)

Rosita Faingold de Villagra (cousin of the author's father)

Rubén Saferstein (author's friend)

Teresa Faingold de Korbenfeld (author's aunt)

About This Book

T his is a chronicle of the author's family's experiences that took place before, during, and after the last military dictatorship in Argentina (1976–1983). The author has used his diaries, interviews recorded in Argentina, Uruguay and Israel, documents and pictures given to him by his family and friends and has studied the works of political scientists, historians and journalists to write this book. He begins this book with his family's history from the time when they immigrated to Argentina towards the end of the 19th century. Then, using his family's history as a background, he discusses his family's experience before his parents' decision to move to Israel in 1976, the decision he made to live by himself in Denmark towards the beginning of 1978, his return to Argentina at the beginning of 1979 to comply with military service at Battalion 3 of the Marine Infantry and his return to Israel in 1980.

During the seven years of the Argentine dictatorship, over thirty thousand people "disappeared" or were murdered by military and paramilitary groups. Approximately two million Argentines went into exile to avoid being casualties of the state-sponsored terrorism. Just like the "disappeared", the exiles were also victims of the "Dirty War" of the military against its own country. It is important to safeguard the stories of those years of the military repression, and to reproduce testimonies of the damage caused to the victims, including those who left to avoid being murdered by the military. The object of this book is to contribute to the collective memory of Argentina and the concept of *Never Again*, so that this idea can be more of a reality than a dream.

About the Author

Author/Editor Bio:

Eduardo D. Faingold is Professor of Spanish and Linguistics at the University of Tulsa. He received numerous grants and fellowships from *the National Endowment for the Humanities, the German Science Foundation, the DAAD, the South African Science Foundation, the Salzburg Seminar, the Max Planck Institute for Evolutionary Anthropology in Leipzig, and the Max Planck Institute for Comparative Public Law and International Law in Heidelberg.* Faingold is the author of numerous articles in refereed journals, including *Language Problems and Language Planning, Journal of Pidgin and Creole Languages, International Journal of Bilingual Education and Bilingualism, Journal of Psycholinguistic Research, International Journal of Jewish Education Research, Estudios de Lingüística Aplicada,* and *Papiere zur Linguistik.* He is the author of eleven books in the areas of language acquisition and learning, bilingualism, creole linguistics, Spanish grammar, language and the law, and immigration/refugee studies, most recently *Language rights and the law in the United States and its territories* (Lexington Books, 2018), *Language rights and the law in the European Union* (Palgrave Macmillan, 2020), and *Language rights and the law in Scandinavia* (Palgrave Macmillan, 2023). He is currently working on a new book dealing with aspects of the acquisition, teaching, history, grammar, and politics of Jewish languages.